MYSTERIES OF
WITCHCRAFT
AND
THE OCCULT

MYSTERIES OF
WITCHCRAFT
AND
THE OCCULT

Robert Jackson

THE
APPLE
PRESS

A QUINTET BOOK

Published by The Apple Press
6 Blundell Street
London N7 9BH

ISBN 1-85076-332-1

This book was designed and produced by
Quintet Publishing Limited
6 Blundell Street
London N7 9BH

Creative Director: Terry Jeavons
Designer: Chris Dymond
Project Editors: Damian Thompson, Caroline Beattie
Editor: Henrietta Wilkinson
Picture Researcher: Liz Eddison
Illustrator: Ivan Hissey

Typeset in Great Britain by
Central Southern Typesetters, Eastbourne
Manufactured in Hong Kong by Regent Publishing Services Limited
Printed in Hong Kong by Leefung-Asco Printers Limited

Contents

CHAPTER 1

The Curse of Voodoo

For many people, the word 'voodoo' immediately conjures up a picture of the zombies, the most publicized aspect of this ancient African religion, brought to the island of Haiti by the first batches of slaves during the seventeeth century. Zombies are people whose 'deaths' have been recorded, and whose burials have been witnessed, and who are nonetheless found living months or years later in a state of mindlessness. They are not legend, but fact, as anyone who has made a serious study of voodoo will testify.

Zombies are created by voodoo sorcerers, skilled in the preparation of drugs which induce a state of coma indistinguishable from death. In one famous case, the daughter of a leading French family on the island vanished from her home, only to be found years later in a hovel in a native village, a mindless creature dressed in rags. Nothing could be done to restore her sanity, and she ended her days shut away in a convent.

BELOW
The scars of voodoo and the white man's exploitation are not apparent in this nineteenth-century pastoral engraving of Haiti.

OPPOSITE
Devotees of voodoo who were executed for cannibalism by the French colonial authorities in 1865.

The subject of zombies was treated so seriously by Haiti's old colonial authorities that a special law was drawn up relating to them. Article 246 of the old Penal Code states:

'Also to be termed intention to kill, by poisoning, is the use of substances whereby a person is not killed but reduced to a state of lethargy, more or less prolonged, and this without regard to the manner in which the substances were used or what were their later results. If, following the aforesaid state of lethargy the person is buried, then the attempt will be termed murder.'

In spite of much research, no-one – except the *hungans*, the voodoo priests themselves – knows exactly how a person is transformed into one of the living dead. But when there is a reason to fear that a corpse may become a victim, his family can take certain measures to ward off this awful fate. The usual method is to 'kill' the person a second time by shooting or strangling him, or to bury him face down, with a dagger in his hand, so that he may kill any sorcerer who tries to disturb his rest. Sometimes, too, the mouths of the undead are sewn up, as it is believed that a corpse can only be raised if it answers its own name.

Once raised by the mysterious powers of the sorcerer, the zombie hangs in the narrow twilight zone between life and death. It can move, eat, speak, hear what is said to it – but it remains completely unthinking and unaware of its condition, and it has no memory of its former life. The zombie's value is as a source of cheap labour; it can be exploited mercilessly and fed on a few scraps of food every day.

Zombies are recognized by their glassy stare and their slow, lethargic movements. Their voices, too, are flat and nasal, an echo of the voices of the *Guede*, the voodoo religion's spirits of death. Only one restriction is imposed on anyone who owns a zombie; the creature must never be given salt. If a zombie eats salt, it becomes instantly aware of its condition – with disastrous consequences. It becomes possessed with a terrible desire for revenge, killing its master and destroying his property before going in search of its grave.

The zombies are, perhaps, the most dramatic manifestation of the voodoo sorcerer's art. However, voodoo magic does not originate exclusively in Africa; it has been influenced to a great extent by superstitions that originated in France, and which were subsequently 'borrowed' by voodoo.

There can be no doubt that the black magic of voodoo is behind at least a percentage of the mysterious deaths that occur in Haiti every year. As in medieval Europe, spells intended to kill or harm a person in some way are cast with the aid of an effigy or image symbolizing that person, although in Haiti this kind of

witchcraft often takes an unusual form. The sorcerer usually sits in front of a bucket of water, muttering incantations designed to lure the spirit of the person he wishes to kill into the water. As soon as he sees the person's image reflected in the water, he stabs it – and if he has been successful, the water turns red.

Haitian sorcery, however, is a two-edged weapon. The family of someone who has fallen victim to black magic are in honour bound to hit back at the person who originated the spell by similar methods – and they will spare neither time nor expense until they have their revenge. The originator of a spell lives in constant fear that God will not condone his crime and withdraw the protection of the family *loa*, or spirits, leaving the person defenceless against the magic of his opponents.

The voodoo sorcerer normally performs his spells at a lonely crossroads or in a cemetery. The actual casting of death-spells is shrouded in secrecy, but the voodoo magician has several lethal supernatural weapons he can use to achieve his aim. The most terrible practice is called 'the sending of the dead', in which the spirits of the dead are sent to harass some unfortunate person. It almost invariably produces fatal results, with the afflicted person growing steadily thinner and spitting blood – unless he manages to

find a more powerful sorcerer who is capable of making the dead spirit release its terrible grip.

Whether an invocation works or not depends on the approval of the dreaded Baron Samedi, the Lord of the Dead. The priest strikes the altar consecrated to the god three times with his knife, crying out the god's name with each blow. He is then possessed by Baron Samedi, who speaks through his mouth and orders whoever is appealing to him for help to bring an offering of fruit to the cemetery at midnight. The client also takes a handful of earth for each of the dead spirits he wishes to send and must sprinkle it on some path frequently trodden by his victim. As soon as the victim walks over this earth, the dead enter his body and he is doomed.

In one respect, the voodoo cult stands out from every other form of occult worship in the world. To practise voodoo successfully one has to be a Christian – and not only a Christian, but a Roman Catholic. The voodoo worshipper who answers the throb of the drums and attends the ancient ritual in some forest clearing every Saturday night firmly believes that he is acting like a good Christian – and would be plunged into the depths of despair if, on the following Sunday morning, he were to be refused Holy Communion at Mass.

This strange paradox is caused by the fusion of African and European beliefs. The average Haitian follows the rites of the Roman Catholic Church devoutly, as he has been brought up to do since infancy, but voodoo provides him with a more alive, physical belief which conveniently fills the gaps left by Christianity.

This explains why the voodoo gods share a common identity with so many Christian saints. St Patrick, for example, doubles as Damballah-wedo, the serpent-god, because legend has it that Patrick expelled all snakes from Ireland; St James the Great is also Ogu-feraille, the warrior-god, while St John the Baptist is Shango, the storm-god, and there are dozens of others. Voodoo has also borrowed heavily from the liturgy of the Church; listening to voodoo ritual is almost, in places, like listening to the Mass.

It took a long time for the Church to wake up to the fact that Christian religion in Haiti was becoming synonymous with voodoo practice. In fact, the first official attempt by the Church to suppress voodoo was not made until 1896, when the Bishop of Cap Haitien organized a 'league against voodoo'. The campaign was unsuccessful and was quickly forgotten, but in 1941, when Elie Lescot was President, a more determined effort was made to stamp out the ancient religion. The anti-superstition crusade that followed was in reality a form of Inquisition, in which all members of the faithful were required to take an oath never to take part in voodoo ceremonies again.

Not unnaturally, this caused great indignation among the people – particularly in a region known as the Marbial Valley, where two priests, one French and the other Haitian, persecuted voodoo with a ferocious and medieval hatred. With a band of followers, the priests visited every house in their parish, smashing every object that was thought to have an occult significance and cutting down sacred trees – the homes of benevolent *loa*.

FACING PAGE
The mist-shrouded and mysterious land of Haiti. Its wooded valleys conceal their age-old secrets of witchcraft to this day.

BELOW
Surrealistic painting of a voodoo initiation ceremony by Rose-Marie Desruisseaux.

The effect was dramatic. Dozens of people became possessed by home-less *loa*, even in the Catholic Church itself, and had to be exorcized on the spot. On one occasion, a group of screaming women were dragged before the priests, accused by neighbours of belonging to the feared 'Sisterhood of the Werewolves'. They too were exorcized. The priests then ordered that all the big crosses in the family burial grounds must be uprooted, since voodoo rituals were held in front of these crosses.

The wooden crosses were piled in a heap and set on fire, and at that moment several people began to twist and turn in a frenzy, screaming that they were possessed by Baron Samedi and the hosts of the dead. No amount of exorcism could drive out the spirits, which mocked the priests and prophesied calamities to come. It came as no surprise to the inhabitants of the valley when, in the following year, the Marbial Valley was hit by the worst drought in living memory.

The battle against the forces of voodoo resulted in a technical victory for the priests and their associates – for a time, at least. Then, in the 1960s, came the anti-Catholic campaigns of the late President François Duvalier, the feared 'Papa Doc', himself an adherent of voodoo. The campaigns were implemented by his secret police, the 'Tonton Macoute', and ended with the Catholic clergy in Haiti being decimated by exile. Voodoo once again had a strangle-hold on the people.

In spite of claims made by the clergy and others who have come into direct contact with voodoo, the idea that the old religion – which had its early origins in Madagascar – is based on cruelty and blood sacrifice is largely a myth. The fact that the myth is more

RIGHT
The face of the living dead – a female victim of voodoo, hovering in the narrow zone between life and death.

FACING PAGE,
François Duvalier, the late president of Haiti. The infamous 'Papa Doc' was an adherent of voodoo, and the Catholic Church in Haiti was decimated under his regime.

PAPA DOC'S RISE TO POWER

During the years the late Haitian President, François Duvalier, worked as a doctor in the countryside – and where, by sheer strength of character, he accomplished tremendous medical reforms almost single-handed – he knew many voodoo priests and attended their ceremonies. He won their support for his political ambitions by promising them rich rewards when he attained power. After he had become the all-powerful ruler he cunningly arranged for insidious stories about his black magic prowess to circulate among the superstitious people. There were stories of weird and terrifying ceremonies taking place in the presidential palace, and led by Duvalier; of demon spirit gods being summoned to his aid; of his habit of reaching policy decisions by studying the entrails of animals. He called his political police 'Tonton Macoute' – 'Uncle Hears Me' – after the voodoo bogeyman who kidnaps children.

ABOVE
This stylized painting by Camy Rocher depicts a voodoo ritual in progress. The attendants and sorcerer are preparing to sacrifice a goat in order to invoke a tree spirit.

universally accepted than reality is the fault of a few isolated cases which, taken together and quoted in almost every work dealing with the subject, have given voodoo a bad name.

Of these incidents, the most notorious is the so-called Bizoton affair, which took place in 1863. A man called Congo Pelle, whose sister was a voodoo witch, made plans to sacrifice his niece to a voodoo god. The child was kidnapped, strangled, cut up and eaten in a bloody ceremony, and a few days later another little girl suffered the same fate. The criminals were eventually captured, tortured and executed – the damage they had done to voodoo was irreparable.

Nevertheless, there is no denying that voodoo is based to a great extent on fear – and above all fear of the dark, of things unseen. The average Haitian peasant will not venture out alone after dark unless it is absolutely necessary – and it is not ghosts or evil spirits he fears as much an encounter with the 'hairless pigs' or 'Grey Ones', bands of sorcerers who are dedicated to black magic and who are so powerful that they form a kind of voodoo mafia.

The 'Grey Ones' cannot be identified by any badge or mark; they are often well-to-do people, living outwardly normal lives among their neighbours. If they are found out, the consequences can be terrible – for them. One merchant whose secret activities were discovered quite by chance was torn limb from limb by a crowd of enraged neighbours.

The 'Grey Ones' hold their Sabbats (gatherings) on certain nights of the week, which they say belong to them alone. They are summoned to the meeting-place by the sharp rhythm of a small drum, which – although it can be heard at great distances by the sorcerers – is said to be inaudible to the uninitiated.

They wear long red or white robes and a variety of headgear, including the traditional conical hat of the witch. In a winding procession, carrying candles, they go to some lonely crossroads where they hold a ceremony in honour of Maître-Carrefour, the Grand Master of Sorcery, asking him to bless their activities. They then move on to a cemetery, where Baron Samedi is invoked, before lying in wait for some unsuspecting victim, who is not

BELOW
A carnival scene in Haiti in the nineteenth century. Virtually all of these people would have been voodoo adherents.

RIGHT
*The Haitian revolution of
23 August 1791 was put down by
the French authorities with great
brutality and served to strengthen
the forces of voodoo.*

always killed. If he seems a likely candidate, he is given the choice of joining the sorcerers as a neophyte – or suffering an unspeakable death. Not many refuse the invitation.

Ordinary people may obtain a degree of immunity from sorcerers by having one of their souls – each person has two, according to voodoo tradition – extracted from the body by way of the head. A *hungan* places a lock of hair from his client's head in a bottle, together with nail-clippings and tufts of hair from the various parts of the person's body. A package of food, mostly bread and sweets soaked in white wine, is then clamped on the person's head. A white cockerel is cooked and eaten by the person's family, great care being taken not to break any of the bones. These are gathered up after the meal and buried under the bed of the person under treatment.

The main danger attached to this process is that the bottle containing the person's soul might fall into the hands of an enemy of an evil sorcerer – in which case the person is as good as dead, for not even the most powerful *hungan* can help him to regain mastery of the lost soul.

Belonging to a voodoo cult can mean an enormous financial strain, and yet voodoo fills an important gap in Haitian peasant society. In a country where organized medical services are practically non-existent outside the capital, Port-au-Prince, it is the considerable skill of the *hungan* that sees the peasant through pain and sickness. And apart from that, voodoo is a rich source of entertainment. Many people feel that its continued practice is entirely justified, despite its darker side, by the fact that it has enabled the people of Haiti to carry on African traditions and culture. In fact, if it had not been for voodoo, many ancient African rituals would have been lost forever.

But voodoo as a religion is no longer African, however. It is sheer paganism and black magic, dark legend and fairy-tale – and it belongs to the western world. This, perhaps, is where its true fascination lies.

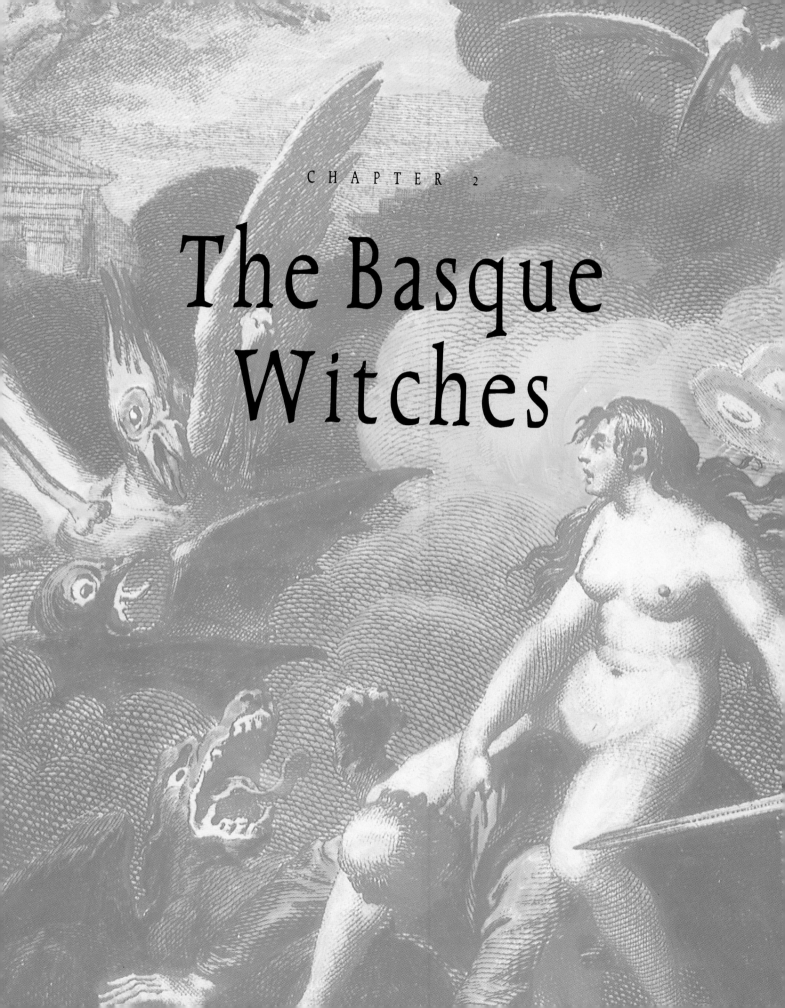

CHAPTER 2

The Basque Witches

T hirteen-year-old Isabel Garcia had a strange story to tell. According to her, she was washing her clothes in a stream one day when she was approached by an old woman named Maria de Illara, who had offered her money if she would do some errands for her that afternoon. The girl agreed, and Maria de Illara said that she would call for her.

But the woman had not returned in the afternoon. It was night when she came, when Isabel was in bed with her mother. The girl told how Maria had dragged her out of the bed and over to the window, where some strange ointment had been rubbed under her armpits; the next moment, with Maria's hands firmly on her shoulders, she had flown out of the window and away across the rooftops until finally she came to a hill called Jaizquibel, near the chapel of Santa Barbara.

There were others there, too. It had been obvious, the girl said, that a Sabbat was being held, and went on to describe the meeting.

BELOW
A witches' sabbath. Hand-coloured engraving by Ziarnko, from Pierre l'Ancre's Tableau de l'Inconstance des Mauvais Anges et Demons, *1610 edition.*

The Devil, in the form of a man but with three horns and a tail, was sitting on a golden throne; the girl was presented to him by Maria, and the Devil urged her to renounce Jesus Christ, the Virgin Mary, the Holy Fathers of the Church and her godparents.

The members of the coven had then begun to dance to the accompaniment of drums, fifes and flutes. All the dancers wore masks, but Isabel recognized several of them. She also said that she had seen the Devil having sexual intercourse with women, girls and young men, and he had given her an apple which she had eaten. Two hours later, Maria de Illara had taken her home again. Her mother was still asleep and had not noticed her absence.

Another 13-year-old girl, Maria de Alzueta, also testified that she had been kidnapped and taken to a Sabbat in much the same manner as Isabel. In fact, her story was very nearly identical.

The year was 1611. The place: Fuenterrabia, a town in the heart of the mysterious Basque country on the Spanish side of the Pyrenees. The two girls made their sworn statements in front of the town council, who gave orders for the women mentioned in the girls' accounts to be arrested.

There were four of them, and they promptly denied all the charges. One of them, Inès de Gaxen, had already been tried for witchcraft in France, but had been found not guilty. Soon after the four had denied the charge, however, 69-year-old Maria de Illara asked to make a further statement – and this time she confessed to being a witch. She admitted that she had become a witch 48 years earlier, while in the service of one Joan de Tapia.

Maria confessed that she had bewitched several children, including Isabel Garcia, and that she had had intercourse with the Devil scores of times. After her statement, more children came forward and laid accusations against the four women. Two more subsequently confessed; the sole exception was Inès de Gaxen.

THE BASQUES' LOST HERITAGE

The Basque language, or Euskara, to give it its proper name, is the oldest living tongue in Europe. No one has yet been able to fathom its origin; some scholars believe that it arose in the Caucasus, a traditional haven for wandering peoples and lost languages, while others claim that it is an African language. Romans, barbarians and Saracens all failed to subdue the Basques, who are hardy fighters and are thought to have allied themselves with the Saracen invasion of Spain. In fact, they may have been the 'Sarrasins' who mauled Charlemagne's rearguard at the Pass of Roncesvalles in 778. It is even conceivable that the Basques – and the pagan rituals associated with their traditions – may be Punic in origin, arising from the ruins of the Carthaginian Empire.

All four witches were imprisoned, while the town council sent full details of the affair to Salazar de Frias, an Inquisitor of the Church, who was carrying out investigations into the alleged activities of witches in the mountainous areas of Navarre. Surprisingly, de Frias didn't seem to be interested. He wrote a long letter to the council, giving permission for the witches' belongings to be returned to them – and that was all. The council had no alternative but to release the four women, on condition that they left Fuenterrabia and never returned.

Salazar de Frias's lenient attitude was surprising, because in the previous year he had been a leading figure in a great purge of witches that had taken place at Zugarramurdi, in the north-western region of Navarre. This was one of the leading centres of witchcraft in the Basque country, and Sabbats were held in a place known as the 'Field of the He-Goat' just outside the town. There was a sheer cliff at one end of the field, and in it was a large cave which the satanists used as their temple. A river known as the Stream of Hell ran through this cave, and above it, on a ledge, stood the Devil's throne.

The witches held ordinary ritual meetings every Friday night throughout the year, but Black Mass was celebrated on the night before certain Christian festivals such as Christmas, Easter and Whitsun. The Devil himself was said to officiate on these occasions, assisted by his acolytes, and the Black Mass was said in the Basque language instead of Latin.

Contemporary accounts attribute a great variety of crimes to the Basque witches and the 'Devil', or high priest, who presided

FACING PAGE
This anonymous hand-coloured engraving of the eighteenth century is said by some to represent a nightmare, and by others to depict a witch with her demons, tormenting a lost soul.

RIGHT
A folk dance in the streets of Bilbao. The origins of these dances, like those of the Basques themselves, are lost in the mists of antiquity.

over their gatherings. Zugarramurdi was not very far from the coast, and the witches were frequently accused of conjuring up the terrible storms that swept the Bay of Biscay, sending many a sailor to his death. They were also accused of producing freak storms to ruin the harvest, but these could be silenced simply by pronouncing the name of Jesus. In the early autumn, when a southerly wind called the Egoa was blowing, the witches were also said to use poisonous powders to ruin the crops. Even today, the Egoa is known as the *Sorguin Aizia*, or 'Wind of the Witches'.

The Zugarramurdi witch trial ended on 8 November, 1610, and the witches heard their sentences, which were characteristically harsh. Eighteen repented and were reinstated in the Church, but seven others were burned at the stake, as were the effigies of five more who had died under torture.

A seventeenth-century historian who recorded the alleged activities of witches in the Basque country, Frenchman Pierre de Lancre, acted as chief judge in a series of trials in the Labourd

RIGHT
Hand-coloured print after Jose de la
Pena, based on a painting in the
witchcraft section of the Basque
Museum in Bayonne. The image is
based on the trial records of de
Lancre.

region of the Pyrenees. He was a harsh judge, but nevertheless he was a talented and intelligent chronicler – and his works contain valuable descriptions of satanic ceremonies.

De Lancre believed that Satan had chosen the Basque region to be the centre of witchcraft in Europe because it stood apart from the political and religious influences of the rest of Europe. Even the language spoken by the people, a language that bore no comparison to any other – and whose origin is still unknown today – helped to increase the isolation. The Basques were turbulent and restless, fond of magic and wild dancing – and were very superstitious into the bargain. Apart from that, the great majority of the menfolk were seafarers, absent from home for lengthy periods – and while they were away the Devil found it an easy matter to sow the seeds of evil among the women.

When de Lancre and his 'witchfinders' arrived in the Basque country from the French side of the frontier, thousands of people fled southwards into Spain to escape the persecution. They were the lucky ones. De Lancre described how, when he arrived in one parish, the local witches asked the Devil for special protection against the bonfires that were being lit all over the country by de Lancre and his men for burning witches. The bonfires, at least, were real enough.

During his investigations, de Lancre was scandalized by the number of priests who confessed to being implicated in satanic activities. One old priest – so old, in fact, that he probably didn't know what he was saying – stated that he had worshiped the Devil until 15 or 16 years earlier, when he had decided to abandon satanism and return to the fold of Christianity.

The priest admitted to have taken part in the foul and evil rituals of the Sabbat, and signed three confessions. As de Lancre revealed that he had been tortured, the poor old man would probably have confessed to anything if only it meant that his agony would be at an end. The confession was his death-warrant; he was defrocked and then burnt to death in his own town as 'an example to good Christians'.

After the execution, many priests joined the ranks of those who were already on the run from de Lancre's witch-hunting activities. Nevertheless, de Lancre succeeded in catching seven of the leading priests of the Labourd region. Three of these were found guilty of celebrating the Black Mass and were executed. One of the men, an independent chronicler notes, had not cele-brated anything for years because he was completely mad – but it seems that neither de Lancre nor his associates noticed this fact. Or if they did, they ignored it.

De Lancre's 'commission' employed the same techniques as witchfinders elsewhere in Europe. Their accusations and trials were based on denunciations made by children, senile people, those who harboured grudges against individuals and suspects who had been tortured until they were insane. The information de Lancre gathered in this way must have been made even more suspect by the fact that he spoke no Basque.

Among de Lancre's accomplices were several quack doctors who claimed to be expert at discovering 'witch-marks' on the bodies of their unfortunate victims. With the assistance of people such as these, de Lancre managed to 'prove' that more than 3,000 people in Labourd had the witch's mark – in other words, an insensitive spot on the body that registered no pain when a needle

was plunged into it. Yet although he referred to it frequently, de Lancre was unable to prove that the 'mark of the toad' existed in the alleged witches' eyes, either. Yet this lack of firm evidence did nothing to prevent him from sending his unfortunate victims to the flames, witch-marks or not.

Despite the havoc he wrought, and the innocent people he condemned to death, de Lancre was without doubt one of the most ludicrous witchfinders in Europe. Even the brutal and ignor-ant Matthew Hopkins, England's Witchfinder General, was

motivated by greed; he received a fixed sum for every witch he convicted. De Lancre, on the other hand, had no such motive. He sowed a trail of terror and bloodshed throughout the Basque country because he genuinely believed that every dark shadow concealed a witch.

Whether the Basque country was in fact the hotbed of witchcraft that de Lancre and the others claimed it to be is a matter for conjecture. The fact remains, however, that witchcraft continued to be practised long after the seventeenth-century witch trials, and is still practised in many a Pyreneean village today. Some parts of the Basque country are said to produce more witches than others. Superstition still holds the Basque peasants in fear of witchcraft, and strangers – particularly if they speak Basque fluently – are looked upon with suspicion in many of the more remote areas, for it is believed that a witch can be detected by the manner in which he or she speaks. Another belief is that a person can become a witch simply by possessing something that has belonged to a known sorcerer, or by performing certain acts – such as walking round a church three times. In addition, if a person is touched by a dying witch, the witch's powers are transmitted to that person.

The power of the witch that is most feared in the Basque country is the Evil Eye, and Basque folklore is rich in stories about this belief. One story, dating from the early part of this century, tells how several children living in a street in Fuenterrabia fell sick. An old woman who walked along the street every morning was blamed for putting the Evil Eye on them. The angry mothers of the children caught the old woman and were about to burn her when she was saved in the nick of time by some men who happened to be passing.

According to Basque tradition, the best way to lift a spell is to make a careful inspection of mattresses in the house where the spell is working, since spells are thought to be carried in little tufts of wool taken from the stuffing of a mattress and fashioned into the shapes of animals. If the spell is a relatively unimportant one, a pair of scissors placed on the mattress in the shape of a cross will ward it off; if it is a powerful one, the whole mattress must be burnt to a cinder.

RIGHT
Many witch-jars have been found, containing such things as urine, nail-clippings and other personal objects used in magical enchantments.

OVERLEAF
The rolling Basque country. It is hard to believe that black arts could flourish amid such beauty.

According to the Basques, there are various ways in which one can tell whether a witch is near at hand; when a cock crows at an unusual time, for example. When that happens, the best thing to do is throw a handful of salt on the fire, or cross the fingers of both hands. Many Basques will never go near a cave at night, because caves are the traditional meeting-places of witches. Other meeting-places are dolmens – stone monuments erected by the country's ancient inhabitants – freshwater springs and steep hillsides where streams flow. The idea that the ceremonies of witchcraft must be practised near water is not just a Basque superstition; it extends throughout the world.

Throughout the centuries, witchcraft has been the strongest among peoples who are devoutly religious. This is true of the Basques, and there can be little doubt that as long as the Basques retain their old traditions and some measure of independence, witchcraft will continue to be practised in the Pyrenees.

But the witchcraft of the Basques is unique in Europe, for it is not confined to a particular cult. There is magic behind every tree, in every stream – and it is in the hearts of the people themselves, no matter how hard they might try to suppress it. For the Basques are an old and mysterious race, and it is perhaps fitting that the Old Religion still finds a place in their ancient culture.

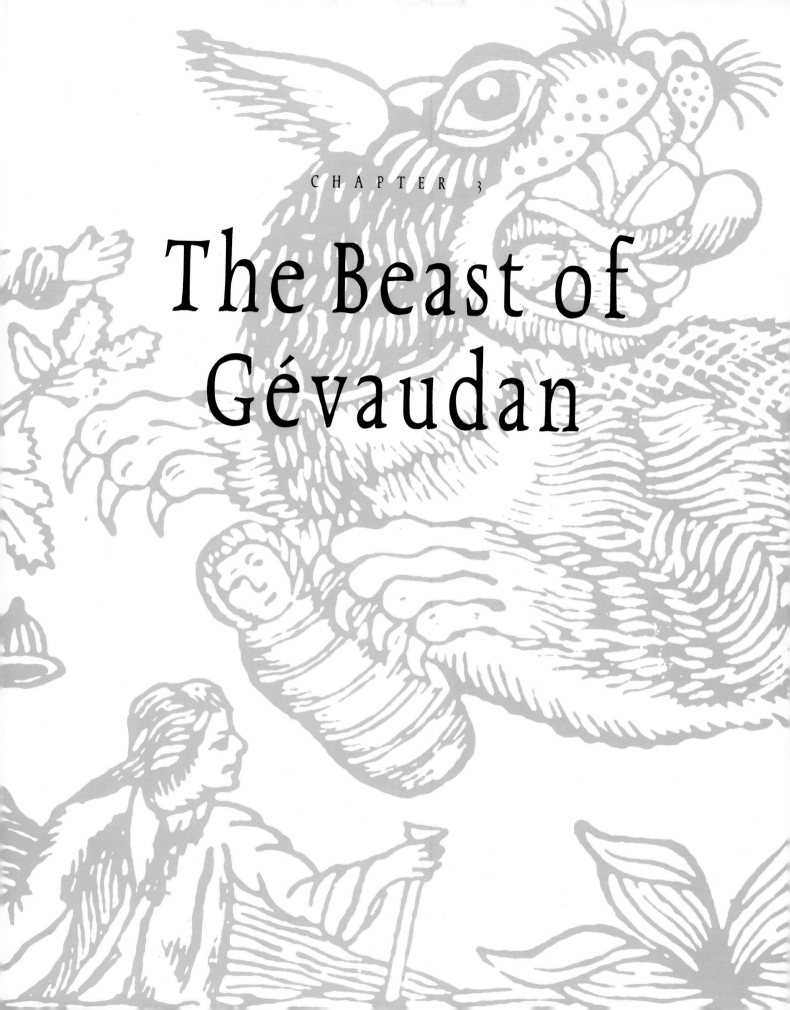

CHAPTER 3

The Beast of Gévaudan

T he word spread like wildfire. Throughout the whole of the Haute Loire region of southern France, people walked in fear and barred their doors against the sinister evil that stalked the land during the hours of darkness. The body of a young girl had been found on the edge of the Mercoire Forest, a few miles southwest of the town of Langogne. She had been literally torn to pieces. The wolf had struck again . . .

It was said that the creature responsible was a devil, that it was not of this earth. It was as big as a bull, with great steel-like claws

and pointed ears that resembed Satan's horns. It was reddish in colour, with a black stripe down its spine – or so people said. Of course, no-one had actually seen the creature and lived to talk about it – but everyone knew somebody who had.

The wolf's first victim was a 14-year-old girl, whose throat was torn out by the creature on 3 July, 1764. A week later, a second girl was killed. In August, the creature almost completely devoured a 15-year-old boy – and in September, its victims included two girls, a woman and another boy. The killings all took place in a heavily wooded area known as Le Gévaudan – and in each case the victim's heart was eaten.

By the end of September, the inhabitants of Le Gévaudan were in the grip of terror. They had never known anything like it. Wolves attacked sheep and other livestock, but rarely did they molest humans – and then only in the depths of winter, when hunger made them ferocious.

In response to a frantic plea by the town's mayor, 40 dragoons arrived in Langogne. For several days they combed the woods of Le Gévaudan, wihtout sighting the wolf. People began to breathe more easily; perhaps the creature had been driven out of the area.

Then, on the first day of October, a 12-year-old girl was attacked and savagely mutilated near her home in the neighbouring region of Saint-Chély d'Apchier. On 7 October, two more girls were killed, followed by a 20-year-old woman a week later.

The Governor of Languedoc issued orders forbidding women and child ren to work alone in the fields, and organized a large-scale hunt for the creature. During the weeks that followed, soldiers and armed peasants killed several wolves – but the beast was not among them. The despairing people of Le Gévaudan were becoming more and more convinced that the creature was supernatural and, therefore, unstoppable.

Heavy snow began to fall, putting an end to the search. But the snow did not deter the beast. On 15 December, it decapitated a 45-year-old woman in Auvergne. Five days later, a young girl suffered

the same fate, and on December 22, the beast was pursued for half an hour by a troop of dragoons – and, according to their report, it literally vanished before their eyes.

Then, on 12 January, 1765, the beast suffered its first defeat. Seven children – five boys and two girls – were guarding a flock of sheep near Villeret d'Apchier. Suddenly, they cried out in terror as they saw a great wolf loping towards them through the long grass.

THE DOG OF DARKNESS

Werewolf legends have been part of European folklore for many centuries, and probably originate in Celtic times, when both wolves and dogs were often associated with evil and disaster. One Welsh legend, for example, tells of Gwyllgi, the Dog of Darkness, a huge animal that stalked the land, paralysing humans with its fearful howl and then destroying them with one glance from its luminous eyes. Norse mythology also tells of a blood-spattered creature called Garmr, which guards the House of the Dead and will do battle with the gods when the Wolves of Hell devour the sun and moon.

ABOVE
Languedoc has always been steeped in the occult. In the Middle Ages the Albigensians, a religious sect who lived in fortresses like this one, were suppressed by a Papal crusade.

A ce Monstre ataqua une femme avec ses trois enfans
en emporta un agé de 18 ans, cette tendre mere animée
du courage maternelle se jeta sur ce monstre qui
la porta un quart d'eure, sur son dos elle fut
heureusement delivré ellé et ses enfans par l'arrivée
d'un homme et de son chien, elle fut recompensé
par sa Majesté

B Cette Bete cruelle devora
le 22 Avril dernier un enfant
de 12 à 13 ans pres le Village
de Prunieres 1764

Ce monstre le 12 Janvier
5 enfans qui gardouent leur
prit un par la tete et l'e
se mirent a la poursuivre
geusement qu'il firent lach
et sauverent leur compagn
donner une recompense

ABOVE	BELOW
This engraving shows the children of Gévaudan gallantly fighting off the beast when it attacked them.	The beast was bowled over by a volley of musket fire, but survived and loped off into the forest.

The beast leaped on one of the boys and began to drag him off. The others gave chase, stabbing at the creature with improvised spears made from knives lashed to the ends of staves. The beast dropped its first victim – who was badly torn about the face, but still alive – and seized another boy by the arm. Led by 12-year-old André Portefaix, the others rushed the creature again, trying to stab it in the eyes. One of them thrust his spear between the beast's jaws, forcing it to release its hold. Portefaix cried 'Save him – or die with him!' and stood over the fallen boy, fending off the creature. At last, bleeding from several deep gashes, it turned and fled. (When King Louis XV heard of André Portefaix's bravery, he rewarded the boy by paying for his education out of the royal purse. Later, Portefaix became an artillery officer.)

However, the people's jubilation was short-lived. Before the end of January, as though enraged by its defeat, the beast claimed five more victims. A fortune was put on the creature's head, the king alone promising 6,000 livres to the person who killed it.

On 7 February, 1765, 20,000 men – everyone capable of carrying a weapon – converged on Mont-Grand, where the beast had last been seen. A troop of dragoons flushed the creature out of its hiding-place and drove it towards the Truyère river, where it was to have been trapped by a strong force of peasants. Unfortunately, the peasants went to the wrong place – and the beast swam across the river and vanished in the woods on the other side.

It was sighted again an hour later, and was bowled over by a volley of musket-fire. It scrambled to its feet again and loped off into the forest – but the pursuers were certain that they had dealt it a mortal blow. No creature of flesh and blood could have survived such a blast of musket-balls. But less than 24 hours later, the beast decapitated another girl. And it left no tracks in the snow around the body.

The superstitious people of Languedoc were now completely resigned to the belief that the beast was an instrument of the Devil, and that no mortal man had the power to destroy it. To make matters worse, the Church stepped in and declared that the wolf had been sent by God to punish the peasants for their sins. A dark aura of gloom hung over the whole land. People went about their tasks furtively, in constant fear. And meanwhile, in March, the beast killed eight more people.

On 7 April, after months of fruitless searching, the dragoons rode away from Langogne. As though to celebrate the occasion, the beast tore out the throat of a 17-year-old shepherdess. On 30 April, after claiming three more victims, the beast was shot twice in the flank by a hunter near Saint-Alban. It escaped, leaving a pool of blood behind it – but just a few hours later, it killed a 40-year-old woman.

The beast grew bolder, prowling along village streets after dark and snarling at barred doors. People whispered that it often walked upright on hind legs, like a man, and now a fearful name sped from mouth to mouth – a name that no-one had dared to utter until now. Werewolf!

Then, in May, came fresh hope. For nearly three weeks, there was no new killing. Perhaps the beast was mortal after all; perhaps a musket-ball had found a vital spot. But the hope was soon

ABOVE
The beast grew bolder, prowling along village streets after dark. Now the people believed that it was a werewolf . . .

dashed. In the evening of 19 May, in Servilanges Wood, the beast struck down an elderly woman and devoured her heart. And on Friday, 24 May, the creature made up for its period of inactivity by killing no less than four people in one day. The terror continued throughout June, when the beast claimed several more victims within sight of their homes.

Meanwhile, King Louis was growing increasingly worried in case the peasants' terror flared into open revolt. In July, he placed the Master of the Royal Hunt – Monsieur Antoine – in command of 20 guardsmen and ordered him to rid Gévaudan of the beast, or die in the attempt. The peasants may have been impressed by the colourful uniforms of Antoine and his guards; the beast apparently was not. As dusk was falling on 9 August, it killed a milkmaid under the very windows of the Château de Besset, where Antoine was staying.

A new and sensational rumour swept the countryside. The beast was indeed a werewolf – and it was said that the man who changed into the savage creature had been captured. His name was Jean Chastel, and he lived the life of a hermit in the forest. He had once been a prisoner of the Moors in North Africa; they had tortured him and turned him into a warped, twisted caricature of a human being. Chastel lived in a part of the forest where the beast was known to lurk, and Monsieur Antoine came upon him

there one day. The man refused to answer any questions; instead, he gave a scream of fury and launched himself at his questioner. He was seized by the guards and spent the next few weeks in prison.

It was rumoured that while Chastel was in prison, the killings stopped. Whether that was true or not, the fact remained that Chastel was released on 1 September – and the following day, the beast tore a young girl to pieces. On 9 September, the mutilated body of another girl was found, and two days later a mule-driver was attacked and killed. On 13 September, a 12-year-old girl vanished completely; all the searchers found were her bonnet and clogs.

Antoine had hunting-dogs brought from Paris and embarked on a new search for the creature, but although he succeeded in killing a large wolf it was clear to all and sundry that it was not the right one. He packed his bags and left Gévaudan for good during early November, in disgrace.

A month later the beast struck again, attacking two shepherdesses and killing one of them. Another girl was killed on 10 December, and 11 days later the beast devoured an 11-year-old named Agnes Mourgues. There was so little left of her that the parish priest thought it was not worthwhile burying the pitiful remains.

The hunt for the creature continued, led now by a young nobleman, the Marquis d'Apchier. With a force of 90 men, he set out every Sunday morning to search the surrounding forest. But always, the party came back empty-handed.

On 4 March, 1766, at dusk, the beast attacked and killed nine-year-old Jean Bergounioux as he was driving his father's cows home for milking. Ten days later, eight-year-old Marie Bompard suffered the same fate in the wood of Liconesse.

As a desperate last resort, the Marquis ordered his men to slaughter dozens of dogs. The carcasses were poisoned and then scattered throughout the woods – but although many animals died a painful death as a result, the beast was not among them. On 17 April, it devoured a six-year-old girl near Clavières, followed by a 10-year-old boy a few weeks later.

There is no record of any killing between 4 June, 1766 – when a young girl was decapitated – and the end of August that year. It seemed as though the beast was growing weary of its fearsome activities; between September 1766 and March 1767, there was an average of only one killing per month. But in March came a brutal re-awakening. By the end of that bloody month, eight people had been killed – all within the area of just one parish. The next month, the horror was repeated in a different parish.

On 19 June, 1767, a small army advanced into the forest once more, determined to pursue the beast until either they or it dropped. And with them went Antoine Chastel, the father of Jean Chastel, who had fled back into his woods to escape the vengeance

FACING PAGE
King Louis XV of
France feared that the
peasants' terror might
flare into open revolt,
and ordered the Royal
Hunt Master to kill
the beast.

LEFT
The snarl of the wolf.
The King's hunters
killed a large creature
like this – but it was
not the beast.

of those who claimed that he was half-man by day, and the beast by night.

As he walked deeper into the forest, following the line of beaters, Antoine Chastel cradled his musket in the crook of his arm. The gun was loaded with a very special ball. He had made it himself – out of silver. Reaching a broad clearing, Chastel sat down on a tree-stump and settled down to wait, leafing through the pages of his prayer-book. The noise of the hunt died away and an uncanny silence fell over the woods.

Suddenly, Chastel sensed that he was being watched. Looking up, he felt a thrill of excitement, mingled with fear. At last, the time had come. Standing motionless on the edge of the clearing was the beast.

Slowly and deliberately, Chastel closed his prayer-book and put it in his pocket. Then, sinking to one knee, he raised his musket and took careful aim at the vulnerable spot just behind the creature's left foreleg. The crash of the musket echoed through the trees. When the smoke cleared, the beast was lying on its side, the grass around it spattered with blood.

Cautiously, Chastel walked over and surveyed the creature. It was big – but not much bigger than an ordinary male wolf. The terrifying thing about it was that even in death it exuded cruelty and ferocity. Its long jaws were equipped with 42 razor-sharp teeth, capable of removing a person's head with a single bite. But Chastel was puzzled by the creature's body. It was not really the body of a wolf; the legs were too thick and the breast too wide. Apart from that, the feet were elongated and had an extra claw. The creature's reddish fur was streaked with strange black bands, and there was a white, heart-shaped mark on its breast.

Today, more than 200 years after Antoine Chastel's silver bullet put an end to the creature's life, mystery still shrouds the true nature of the Beast of Gévaudan. Many people believed that the thing shot by Chastel was not the Beast at all – but the fact remains that there were no more killings after 19 June, 1767.

Just how many people were killed by the beast during its three-year rampage will never be known for certain, but the parish records of the area quote at least 75. Added to this, there were 30 cases of serious injury and mutilation.

Some witnesses maintained that the beast was in fact a were-wolf – but if it was, it had nothing to do with Antoine Chastel's son, Jean. He turned up safe and sound a few days later, his name completely cleared. The beast may have been a mutation – a freak of nature that combined almost human cunning with an exceptionally strong body. Whatever the truth, old legends die hard in superstitious Languedoc – and the legend of the beast that left its mark in blood across the land is no exception.

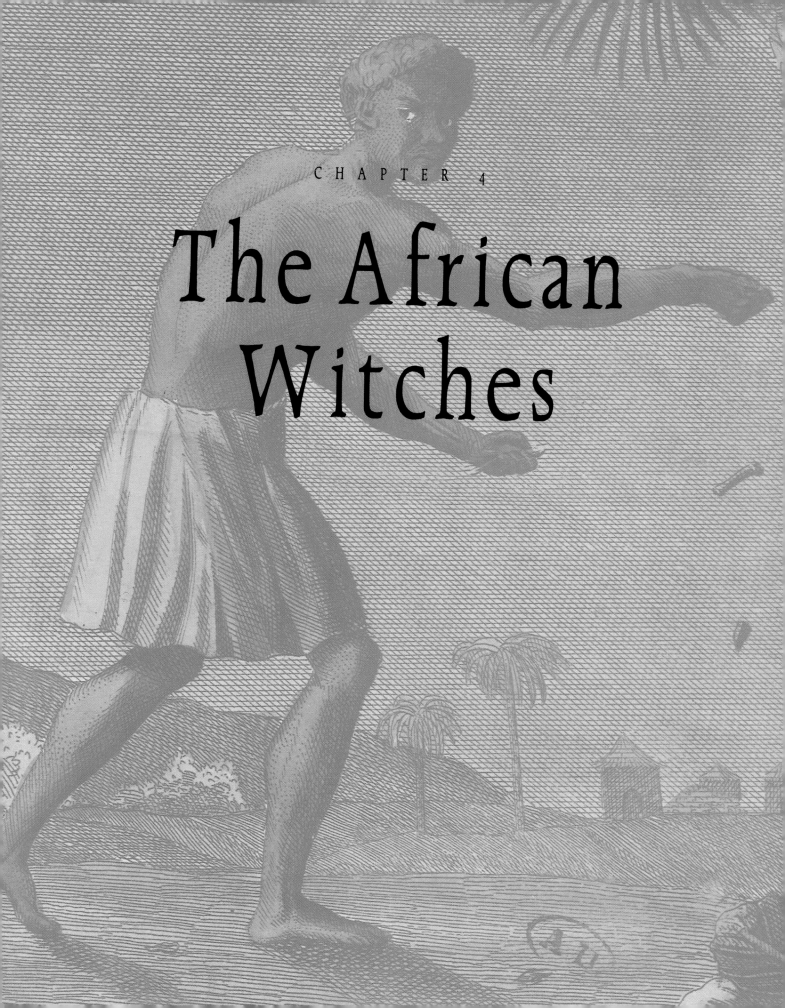

CHAPTER 4

The African
Witches

T he three women stood silently in the dock, never flinching under the prosecutor's impassive gaze. The oldest of the trio was about 70, her eyes radiating malice and hatred. The woman on her right was 30 years younger, and her face was an expressionless mask. Never once, during the entire trial, had she uttered a word. Only the third woman showed any kind of emotion. She was the youngest of the three, not more than 20, and she was visibly bored. Not afraid – just bored. Even though she and her companions had just been found guilty of practising witch-craft and ritual murder . . .

It was like a scene from some dark witch trial of the Middle Ages. But on this occasion the judge was no bloodthirsty witch-finder-general, filled with religious fanaticism and greedy for the bounty he would receive for every witch brought to justice. This was October 1962, the judge was English, and the place was the Tanganyika High Court of Dar-es-Salaam.

LEFT
French painting of a medicine man in Madagascar. Such people still wield enormous power throughout Africa. Madagascar was also the birthplace of voodoo.

ABOVE
*The Ngorogoro crater wood,
Tanganyika, at dawn. Deep among
trees such as these, the black witch
Nyamseni committed her
abominations.*

The trial was the climax of a horror story – a story that had unfolded among the tropical heat and steaming swamps of the Rufiji Delta, where ignorance and fear still held thousands of people in their grip – and enabled monsters like Nyamseni and her evil helpers to rise to power.

Nyamseni was notorious throughout the Delta as a powerful and evil witch. People avoided her sinister, black-robed figure like the plague. In East Africa, witchcraft runs in families; when a witch dies, it is believed that her spirit enters a bottle and stays there until it is reincarnated in another member of her family – who shows that she has been so possessed by twisting and jerking in a fit. She is then initiated into the ancient mysteries by members of the local coven, and takes over the deceased witch's hut and belongings. To refuse to carry on the tradition is to invite a fearful curse. No matter what her circumstances might be, a girl selected to be a witch must abandon her family and friends to enter a world of darkness and fear.

This was the agonizing choice that faced 18-year-old Zabibu, Nyamseni's niece, one day in 1960 when the old witch came to her

and told her that she had been selected for an apprenticeship in black magic At first, Zabibu refused. She had only just married a young man named Màsudi, and she did not want to leave him. For several months she held out, although she was terrified in case Nyamseni called down some awful curse on her husband. For as well as demanding Zabibu's services as a student of witchcraft, the old hag was asking another, more terrible favour of the girl. She wanted to use Masudi for what she called witchcraft practices, and Zabibu knew only too well what that meant. Ritual torture – and perhaps an agonizing death.

By this time, Zabibu was half crazed with fear, but still she bravely resisted the old woman's demands. Then, one day in 1961, following a visit by Nyamensi to Zabibu's hut, the girl's husband fell seriously ill. He collapsed with severe chest pains, and fits of coughing racked his body. The local doctors were unable to do anything to help, and Masudi was rushed to hospital in Dar-es-Salaam. There, he made a rapid recovery – but as soon as he came home he fell ill again.

Soon afterwards, Nyamseni visited the hut again and said that she had put a curse on Masudi. He would never be well again – unless Zabibu consented to become a witch. She would no longer have to depend on Masudi for support. She would be free to do as she liked.

It was too much for Zabibu. Paralysed by Nyamseni's hypnotic gaze, she gave her consent. It was the start of a waking nightmare. A week later, Nyamseni brought Zabibu before a meeting of the witches' coven in the forest not far from the girl's home. The hag told the coven's 18 members that Zabibu had agreed to give up her husband to be slaughtered and his body used for the preparation of horrible potions.

The girl's initiation into the realms of horror began in earnest a few days later when Nyamseni took her to an assembly of three covens in another village. Shortly after they arrived, the witches

EVIL SPIRITS

African mythology abounds with the spirits of good and evil. Evil spirits (often harbingers of death), who tend to be more colourful, are constantly striving to hinder the good spirits. Central to African mythology, though, is a rather vague supreme being, the creator of all things, whose name varies from region to region. There is a strong belief throughout Africa in life after death, and the spirits of the dead are a potent force in the practice of magic. One especially unpleasant spirit, Ngworekara, rules over the spirits of the dead. Bad spirits wander in space, their sole desire to torment the living and eat their hearts.

Marchand d'Esclaves de Gorée

LEFT
Slave traders in Africa, 1796. Such activities undoubtedly played their part in strengthening witchcraft as a means of protection.

moved off into the jungle in a long snake-like procession. Deep among the trees, they halted and formed a circle around something that lay on the ground. Looking closely, Zabibu saw to her horror that it was a young girl. She was stark naked, and although her eyes were wide open in staring horror, she lay quite still. Later, Zabibu learned that her limbs had been paralysed by the effect of a special drug made from herbs.

Three of the witches removed their clothes. As Zabibu watched in fascinated horror, one of them seized the helpless girl's legs and another her arms. A third witch picked up a long, curved knife and severed the girl's head from her body with one swift stroke. Then the arms and legs were cut from the corpse, which was afterwards disembowelled and cut in half. Each of the leading witches present was given a piece of the unfortunate girl's flesh to be dried and ground into powder.

One day, a few months later, Nyamseni's assistant – a 40-year-old woman named Zamlata – gave Zabibu a gourd of 'medicine' and told her to dose Masudi's food with it. The treatment went on for several weeks, and the man grew steadily weaker and more lethargic. It was as though he knew exactly what was happening to him – but he no longer had the will to resist. Then came the day when he finally lapsed into a coma. His body was now ready for the ghastly ritual.

Nyamseni arrived with two other witches, and together they carried Masudi away into the forest. Zabibu was ordered to stay behind. In the solitude of her hut, she broke down and wept as the full significance of what she had done dawned on her. After a while, she pulled herself together and left the hut. She had made up her mind about what she had to do. She ran to her father-in-law and gasped out the full story.

It took Zabibu's father-in-law several minutes to make out just what the distraught girl was saying, but as soon as he learned what had happened to his son, he went to the village headman. The latter was a Christian, and for a long time he had been anxious to obtain evidence that would help bring the witches to justice.

When Nyamseni and Zamlata returned to the village, they were at once seized by a dozen stalwart tribesmen and tied hand and foot. The old witch glared malevolently at the headman as he towered over her, and spat in his face when he demanded to know the whereabouts of Masudi. Turning, the headman barked an order to one of his followers and stared grimly at Nyamseni until the man returned – carrying a pot of pepper. The headman told the witch that unless she revealed where Masudi was hidden, he would throw the pepper into her eyes and blind her for the rest of her life.

It was six months before the witches could be brought to trial. Severe floods swept across the Delta, causing an almost complete breakdown of transport and communications. Finally, the witches appeared before the Utete District Court – only to be remanded to the Tanganyika High Court a week later.

The trial caused a sensation. The courtroom was packed with excited villagers when the charges were read out. Nyamseni, Zamlata and Zabibu were jointly charged with 'making, using, or having in their possession, or representing themselves to possess, an instrument or instruments of witchcraft, and that they also had an intent to cause death, disease or injury to one person, namely Masudi Salum Mwitiko'.

The three were not charged with murder. The doctor's report had not provided conclusive evidence that the kidnapping of Masudi had been directly responsible for his death. As far as the ritual killing of the young girl in the forest was concerned, a full statement accusing Nyamseni had been made by the girl's parents, but had later been unexpectedly withdrawn by them. So had the statements of several other witnesses for the prosecution.

The reason for this was simple. During the six months which had elapsed between Nyamseni's arrest and her trial, her fellow witches had done their work well. The witnesses had been threatened with death, and things worse than death. Even in prison, Nyamseni was still powerful – and black magic continued to have a far greater hold over the people than what was regarded as the white man's law.

Zabibu was the most talkative of the three accused. Quietly, in simple, matter-of-fact tones, she told the court her tale of horror. Then, her statement ended, she seemed to lose all interest in the proceedings. Zamlata, maintaining a stony silence, refused to answer any of the prosecution's questions at all. Nyamseni made only a few surly comments which seemed to confirm what Zabibu had already told.

The three witches seemed to symbolize the power of darkness as, heavily veiled in their black robes, they waited impassively to learn their sentence. When it was passed, the sentence seemed surprisingly light – but it was as much as the law would allow under the circumstances. Nyamseni received six years' hard labour, Zamlata five, and Zabibu three.

The six years were too much for the evil Nyamseni. She died after serving only two. Her assistants were released on time, and returned to their villages. Their fate is not recorded. It is not known whether they were once again accepted into the community, having atoned for their sins – or whether they too met the same fate as their victims, meted out by those whose memories were long.

For the first time, a glimmer of fear showed on Nyamseni's arrogant face. After a moment's hesitation, she told the headman all he wanted to know.

Nevertheless, it took a search party of 50 villagers two days and nights before they found the luckless Masudi. He was conscious, but he could neither move nor speak. Later, in Dar-es-Salaam hospital, doctors were completely baffled by his condition. His face, arms and legs were enormously swollen, yet no trace of poison or infection was found in his blood. They did what they could, but it was too late to save Masudi. He died two weeks later, in fearful pain.

FACING PAGE
A *witchcraft fetish from Zaire,*
formerly the Belgian Congo.
Witches use such charms to work
both good and evil.

Even today, witchcraft – both black and white – is still practised extensively throughout Africa. Basically, it has altered very little in thousands of years. But now, African witchcraft is being employed in a new and sinister role – as a political weapon.

Among the first to employ sorcery in this way were the Mau-Mau, who attempted to topple the government of Kenya in the mid-1950s. Mainly Kikuyu tribesmen, they had to undergo a complex initiation ceremony involving the ritual sacrifice of a goat, with whose blood they were anointed. They had to swear seven oaths, and the penalty for breaking any of them was death. If a Mau-Mau decided to defect, he had to undergo a ritual 'cleansing', or oath-breaking ceremony which was carried out by a medicine man in the pay of the authorities. The Mau-Mau countered this by further black magic, sacrificing a goat near the 'cleansing' centre on the previous night and invoking death on all those who attended the ceremony.

ABOVE
The Mau-Mau recruited most of
their support from Kikuyu tribesmen,
here pictured in a traditional dance.

The Mau-Mau were eventually defeated by the security forces, under British leadership, and by a successful Government propaganda campaign that turned the majority of the people against them, but there is no doubt that the struggle was protracted by the people's terror of their magical 'powers'.

The same was true some years later in central Africa, where rebel tribesmen in Katanga – the Simbas – were spurred on by their witch-doctors to sow a trail of murder and rape across The Congo. Worked up into a trance and plied with drugged beer, the Simbas were told that the witch-doctors' magic made every one of them invincible and immortal. In their case, the magic proved to be worthless against the bullets of mercenaries and United Nations troops, and the Simbas were killed in their hundreds.

In many parts of Africa today, ritual magic is still indivisible from tribal life, and tribalism is indivisible from African politics. The witch-doctor remains a powerful force, often more powerful even than the men who are seeking to bring their states into a Western-dominated world.

BELOW
Plate from the Yoruba tribe of West Africa, engraved with mystic symbols.

CHAPTER 5

The Silver Thread

I n the summer of 1942, a small band of RAF pilots – exhausted by heat and dysentery – took off in their Spitfires day after day against overwhelming odds to defend the island of Malta. One of them, a young flying officer, was ambushed and attacked by several Messerschmitts. His Spitfire was badly shot up and he was wounded.

'I knew that I'd had it,' he said. 'I was resigned to the fact that I was going to die. Then something strange happened. I found myself outside the cockpit, looking down at myself – at my own body, still in the Spitfire. I was attached to it by a slender, silvery thread. It was clearly visible. Then, suddenly, I was back in the cockpit again with a jolt that was physical. I pulled myself together and looked around. My attackers had disappeared. I found that I could just about manage to control my crippled aircraft, and a few minutes later I made a successful forced landing.'

The story is by no means unique. Many other people – the victims of road accidents or other mishaps – have experienced a similar phenomenon. Somehow, part of them – call it the soul, or what you will – has left their physical body for a space of time, and then returned to it. Stranger still, there are many documented cases of people projecting their spiritual self across many miles – a phenomenon known as astral projection.

Take the case of one Mary Smith. She had gone to bed early one evening at harvest-time as she had had a particularly hard day on the farm. She had been asleep for about two hours when suddenly

BELOW
The RAF base at Takali, Malta, under heavy German air attack in 1942.

LEFT
RAF *fighter pilots in their Hurricanes and Spitfires – like this one – fought daily to defend the island. Exhausted, some had strange and supernatural experiences.*

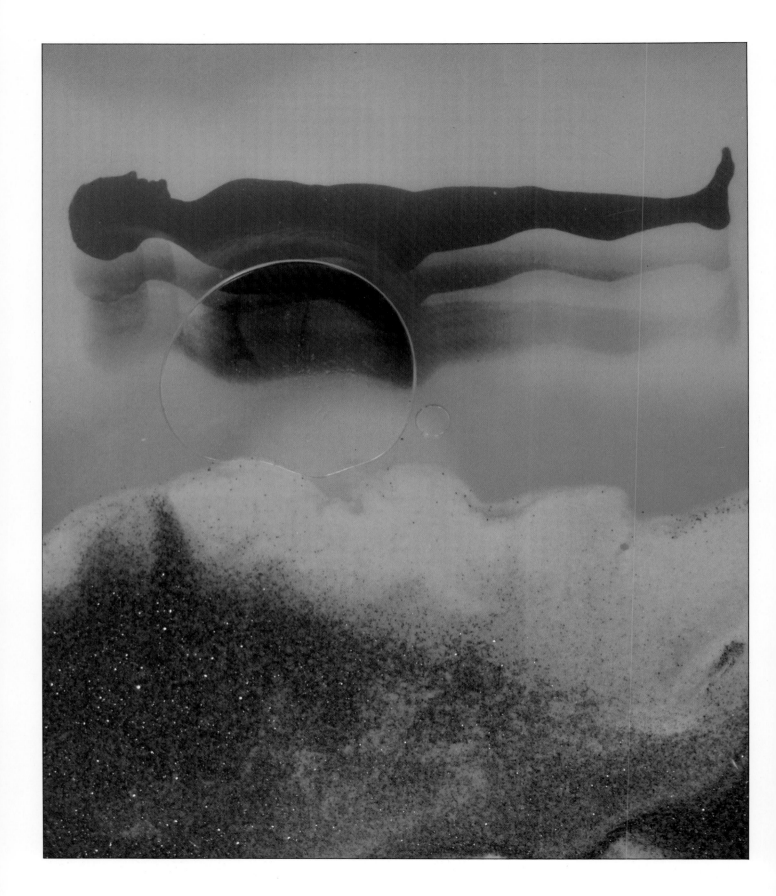

she awoke with a start. Her husband was standing at the foot of the bed, his face and clothing covered in blood. Terrified, she asked him what had happened. He told her not to worry – that he had just had a little accident.

Mrs Smith jumped out of bed to switch on the light, but when she turned round again, her husband had disappeared. Thinking that she had dreamed the whole episode, she went to put out the light. Before doing so, she glanced at the clock on the mantelpiece. It was 10.30 pm. At midnight she woke again. Someone was coming up the stairs. It was her husband. He came and stood at the foot of the bed, and his face and clothing were covered in blood. He spoke exactly the same words as he had done in his wife's 'dream' of an hour and a half earlier.

The two scenes were absolutely identical. Robert added that he had been attacked by two brothers from a neighbouring farm, who bore a long-standing grudge against him. The attack had taken place at exactly 10.30 pm.

This extraordinary story appears in the files of Louisa Rhine, who for half a century studied parapsychology in her husband's laboratory at Duke University in the United States. The story appears under the classification of 'hallucinations', but the word itself does not constitute an explanation. Did Mrs Smith dream? If so, how could she dream, with minute accuracy, future events? Had Robert Smith, during his fight with his assailants, somehow managed to 'project' himself through space to appear simultaneously before his wife?

There are dozens of similar incidents in Louisa Rhine's files. One of them concerns an Ohio housewife whose husband had given her three theatre tickets. She went to see the show with her 12-year-old daughter and a neighbour's little boy. On the way home, they were climbing a flight of steps leading from one street to another, when, on a higher level, the woman suddenly looked up. It was brilliant moonlight, and there at the top of the steps, in

shirt sleeves, she saw her husband looking down benignly at them. She never said a word, but the children both saw the man and pointed at him.

'I thought that he must have left the house in great haste,' said the woman, 'because he wasn't wearing suspenders, and for him that was exceptional. When we got to the top of the steps, he wasn't there any more. We all felt a strange sense of alarm, and

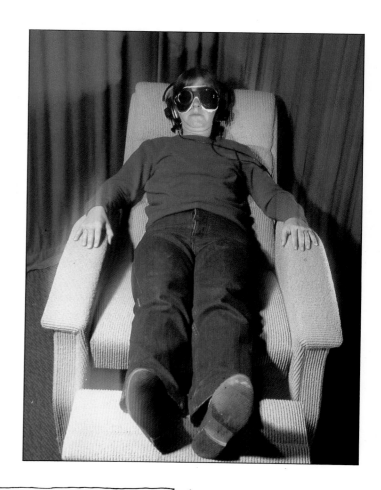

ASTRAL PLANES

Astral projection has been practised by the adepts of many occult groups throughout the world for centuries, and there is strong evidence to show that it works, whether intended or not. Subjects who claim to have attained the state of leaving their physical bodies often find it difficult to describe the splendour of the experience, which projects them into a timeless, spaceless zone of pure magnificence. One subject described it thus: 'There is no ground and no sky. No boundaries of any kind. Everything is open. There are other people there and when we want to communicate we can do so without having to listen, without having to speak . . .'

ABOVE
Out-of-body experiments with coloured glasses and auditory induction through earphones being carried out at Freiburg, Germany, in 1982.

FACING PAGE
This computer-generated image, based on personal accounts of out-of-body experiences, shows the astral body leaving the physical body at death or sleep.

quickened our steps. When we got home, I found my husband asleep in an armchair. He wasn't wearing his suspenders, a fact that struck me at once. But when he awoke, he assured me that he had never left the house for a moment.'

Had she and the children been the victims of an illusion? Hardly. Or had they really seen her husband in the moonlight? While he was asleep, had his spiritual 'double' been taking a quiet stroll around the streets?

At the beginning of 1947, a young American girl named Patricia had stayed in Germany for some time with a friend who was a member of the Forces of Occupation. She then went to England to visit the mother of her friend, whose name was Alan. On Tuesday afternoon, Patricia felt strangely upset and told her hostess that she was worried in case something had happened to Alan. Two days later, she received a letter from the young man, asking whether she had been in Germany recently and what clothes she had been wearing on Tuesday afternoon. She replied, mystified, and from his next letter she learned the facts.

On that Tuesday afternoon, Alan and two other soldiers had been detailed to escort a prisoner to a detention centre 15 miles from their camp. Most of the road was through wooded country, and suddenly they had seen a girl come out of the trees ahead and signal their jeep to stop. They did, and at that precise moment a car turned out of a side-road and sped off at high speed. If they had not stopped, there would have been a serious collision.

The girl who came out of the trees was Pat. Alan recognized her, and so did his companions, who had both met her. They searched for her in vain among the trees, but she had vanished. Somehow, by subconsciously projecting her spiritual body over hundreds of miles, she had managed to appear to her friends in a moment of danger.

For centuries, the mystics of the East have professed mastery over levitation, telepathy, the art of seeing into the future and astral projection. Today, we of the West are gradually coming to admit that the laws of time and space can be overcome by certain individuals, either consciously or unconsciously, and scientists the world over are preoccupied in solving the mystery.

The threads of evidence are scanty, but when gathered together they form an irrefutable picture. One thing is certain: there are people who seem to be able to 'leave their bodies' and project their 'doubles' at will through space, to appear many miles away. Sometimes they have a vague feeling that something out of the ordinary has happened, as in the case of Patricia. In this instance, she was completely unable to control the astral projection.

However, there exist those who can project themselves consciously, as in the following case.

LEFT
A painting of an
astral entity by the
clairvoyant Austin
Spare (1886–1956).
Spare believed that he
was a reincarnation of
the poet, artist and
mystic William Blake.

FACING PAGE
The Italian Army suffered a bitter
defeat at Caporetto in 1917.
Photograph shows Italian infantry
entrenched on a mountainside.

ABOVE
General Cadorna, the Italian
commander at Caporetto,
contemplated taking his own life
after the disaster.

RIGHT
He was dissuaded by Father Pio,
seen here displaying the stigmata,
who appeared to the general in his
astral body.

The Italian Army had suffered a severe defeat at Caporetto. It was November, 1917. The Italian commander, General Cadorna, his troops routed, had retired to his tent and was contemplating suicide. Suddenly, a young monk came in and said:

'Come, General, you must not dream of doing such a thing!' Then he disappeared.

After the war, General Cadorna heard of Father Pio, a priest who bore the stigmata on his flesh – the marks of the nails in Christ's hands and feet. He travelled to southern Italy, to San Giovanni Rotondo, to meet the priest. To his stupefaction, General Cadorna recognized the man who had appeared to him in his hour of distress. The holy man recognized him too, and said:

'You came through it very well, my son.'

Although Father Pio several times demonstrated his power of appearing in two places at the same time, he was never able to explain it – nor indeed did he attempt to do so, mainly because the Church placed a ban of silence on those of its followers who apparently possessed occult powers. That Father Pio had the power of projecting himself at will there can be no doubt, for there have been many witnesses to it.

One such was Monsignor Damiani, Bishop of Salto in Uruguay, who made several trips to Italy to see Father Pio. The Monsignor expressed the wish that he might die at San Giovanni, so that Father Pio could perform the last rites for him. 'No', the priest told him, 'you will die in Uruguay. But I shall be beside you.'

In 1942, the Archbishop of Montevideo was awakened during the night by a messenger who told him that Monsignor Damiani was dying. The Archbishop left at once, but it was too late. On a table near Monsignor Damiani's death-bed, he found a scrap of paper. On it were three simple words, written in the dying man's hand. 'Father Pio came.'

A few years later, in 1949, the Archbishop himself made a pilgrimage to San Giovanni. When he saw Father Pio, he was filled with wonder. For Father Pio was the mysterious messenger who had come to him that night in 1942, with the news that Monsignor Damiani lay dying.

It is quite possible that Father Pio might have been able to enlighten the scientists who were interested in his case, but he would never reveal his secret. Until the day he died, he claimed that his sole mission on earth was to bring help and comfort to those who needed it, and it was to that end alone that he used his miraculous powers. Some scientists, who had made intensive studies of Eastern mysticism, were of the opinion that Father Pio must have reached a high degree of mastery in the technique of meditation, on a parallel with the great Yogis of India. Through his faith, he had acquired supernatural powers.

ABOVE
The American biologist Dr Andreja Puharich recorded the experiences of patients who had out-of-body experiences.

Apart from meditation, there is another way of entering into the detached state of 'mind over matter' necessary for paranormal experiences. Certain early civilizations and peoples – not to mention the witches of medieval Europe – knew of substances, mostly derived from plants, which induced a particular state of mind in the person consuming them. The Mongols and ancient Egyptians, for example, used a substance derived from a certain kind of poisonous mushroom which, when taken, brought on 'dreams that foretold the future.'

One eminent American biologist, Dr Puharich, told of the strange experience of one of his patients, a businessman, whom he was treating with an unspecified type of drug. As soon as he had absorbed the drug, the man lay down. Suddenly, he had the impression of leaving his body and hanging suspended over it, looking down. At first, he put it off as a bad dream induced by the drug, but gradually he found that it was happening when he had not taken the drug at all. Moreover, his 'double' began to journey farther away from his sleeping body. One day, during one of his astral voyages, he met a couple of friends leaving their home. He followed them, and when he met them in the flesh some days later, he was able to give them every detail of their movements that evening.

Researchers such as Dr Puharich are convinced that some day, perhaps in the not too distant future, the key to the whole field of supernormal experiences will be found. The relevant data has been collected over many years, but it is haphazard. Somewhere beneath it all there is an underlying pattern, at present only dimly perceived. But if the tales are to be believed, the wise ones – the witches of old – saw the pattern clearly. Their practices are, at least, worthy of deeper study.

CHAPTER 6

The Witch of Kilkenny

Before she married Sir John le Poer, Lady Alice Kyteler had had three previous husbands. They all had one thing in common. They all died young – and they all died mysteriously.

Lady Alice lived in Kilkenny, Ireland, during the early part of the fourteenth century. She and her family were not popular in the area, partly because they were very wealthy and partly because of their cruelty towards the serfs who were bound to them.

Two of Lady Alice's husbands had been widowers with children, and it was these step-children who were to be responsible for her eventual downfall. The trouble began in 1324, when Sir John le Poer began to suffer from a strange illness – a wasting disease that caused his hair to come out in great tufts and the nails to drop from his toes and fingers. Seeing what was happening to him, Lady Alice's stepchildren began to whisper that it was a mysterious illness just like this that had killed their fathers.

There were other whispers, too – rumours that Lady Alice practised witchcraft – whispers which finally reached Sir John. He demanded the keys to his wife's room, but when she refused to

BELOW
The landscape of Kilkenny, Ireland. Witchcraft began to flourish here in the fourteenth century.

LEFT
Inside Kilkenny Castle, the scene of much magic, intrigue – and perhaps murder.

BELOW
Pope John XXII ordered the formation of what was perhaps to become a greater evil than witchcraft itself – the Inquisition.

give them to him, he took them from her by force. Unlocking the door, he discovered a number of chests that contained phials of evil-smelling liquids and what looked like powdered bones.

For Sir John, the discovery was proof enough that his wife was dabbling in the Black Art. He sent the phials to the Bishop of Ossary – an English Franciscan named Richard de Ledrede – together with a letter written by Lady Alice's stepchildren, accusing her of consorting with the Devil.

The Bishop of Ossary had recently been consecrated by Pope John XXII, who six years earlier had issued the first Papal Bull dealing with sorcery. He had even ordered an enquiry into certain members of his own court, who had been accused of practising magic. This involved charges of raising the dead, causing pain and death by means of images and effigies, and conjuring up demons with the aid of mirrors.

The Pope believed that evil spirits could be imprisoned in rings or mirrors for the purpose of obtaining information about events in either the past or future. To stamp out these practices, he ordered the formation of what was ultimately to become a far greater evil – the Inquisition.

The Bishop of Ossary, eager to please the Pope, duly had Lady Alice arrested, together with 11 others. These were her son by her first marriage, William Outlawe; Robert of Bristol; Alice Faber; John, Helen and Sysoh Galrussyn; William Payne de Boly; Eva de Brounestoun; Annota Lange; Petronella de Meath, Alice's maid; and Petronella's daughter Sarah.

IOANNES XXII PAPA NEPOLITA
NVS CREATVS CARDINALIS A BONIFACIO
IX SEDIT AN V DIES XV VACAVIT SEDES

There were seven formidable charges against them in the Bishop's indictment. First, it was alleged that in the performance of witchcraft they had totally denied the faith of Christ and cast aside the guidance of the Church for long periods, depending on the duration of whatever spells they were weaving. Second it was alleged that they had invoked demons by the sacrifice of living animals, which had been torn apart and the pieces scattered at a crossroads, consecrated by a demon who had told the sorcerers his name was Robert Artisson. And thirdly, Lady Alice and her coven were charged with seeking advice from demons, the premises of the Church being used for this purpose. The charges also included the boilng of a 'noisome brew' in the skull of a beheaded robber; the ingredients included the intestines of cocks, foul worms, nails from corpses, hairs and the brains of boy-children who had died unbaptized – and herbs to add flavour to it all.

From the brew, Lady Alice was said to have made potions that could cause love or hate, or be used for 'harming the bodies of faithful Christians'. On top of it all, there was the allegation that she had disposed of three husbands, and was in the process of getting rid of the fourth when she was found out; that she 'had so infatuated and charmed them that they had given all their property to her and her son and heirs; in so much that her present husband, Sir John le Poer, was reduced to a most miserable state of body by her poisons, ointments and other magical operations; but being warned by her maidservant, he had forcibly taken from his wife the keys of her boxes. Therein was found a wafer of sacra-

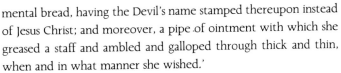

RICH WITCHES

In the Middle Ages in Britain, common folk made little secret of their involvement with witchcraft and suffered because of it, yielding much loot to the Church in the process. Then the Church went in pursuit of more lucrative game, such as Lady Alice Kyteler. She was not alone; Lady Glamis, an ancestor of Queen Elizabeth II, was burned alive as a witch in 1537. The Duchess of Gloucester was condemned as a witch and thrown into the dreaded Bishop's Prison in Peel Castle on the Isle of Man, where she languished in dreadful conditions until her death 16 years later. Her companion Margery, known as the Witch of Eye, was burned at the stake, and another accomplice, Roger Witche, was taken from the Tower of London to Tyburn, where he was hanged, beheaded and quartered.

mental bread, having the Devil's name stamped thereupon instead of Jesus Christ; and moreover, a pipe of ointment with which she greased a staff and ambled and galloped through thick and thin, when and in what manner she wished.'

The indictment also stated that sexual intercourse had taken place between Lady Alice and her familiar, the demon known as Robert Artisson, who sometimes appeared in human shape accompanied by two tall companions with 'dark visages' and sometimes as a cat or shaggy dog. Sacrifice was regularly made to the demon in various ways; in one of them, the eyes of nine peacocks and nine red cocks were placed on a stone bridge at a crossroads. Ointment was then rubbed on a long beam of wood; mounting the beam, Lady Alice and her companions could be carried magically to wherever they desired.

She was also alleged to have 'attracted money to the house of her son, William Outlawe, by taking a broom and sweeping the streets of Kilkenny in the afternoon, raking all the filth towards the door of her son William Outlawe and murmuring secretly these words: "To the house of William, my son, hie all the wealth of Kilkenny town."'

This allegation actually appears in a much later account of the trial, and – since it is extremely hard to visualize a woman of Lady Alice's calibre sweeping the streets in front of a crowd of interested onlookers, muttering to herself into the bargain – it is very probably a fabrication.

Although technically under arrest as far as the Church was concerned, Lady Alice and her accomplices were not imprisoned because in British courts, up to this time, sorcery had not been regarded as a crime that came under the jurisdiction of the Church. The only man with the necessary authority to bring the accused to trial was the Lord Chancellor of Ireland, Roger Outlawe – and he was related to Alice's first husband. He decided to take no action, and tried to persuade the Bishop to drop the charges.

The Bishop refused, and convened an ecclesiastical court at which Lady Alice was excommunicated in her absence. Two days after the court had pronounced its sentence, the Bishop received an important visitor in the shape of Arnald le Poer, the Seneschal (or Steward) of Kilkenny and John le Poer's nephew. The Seneschal made it plain that he did not condone the court or agree with its sentence – at that time, when the Church was virtually the supreme power, excommunication was literally a fate worse than death – and begged the Bishop to reduce the sentence. It was no use. The Seneschal left the Bishopric in a towering rage, shouting threats and swearing that he would have vengeance against the Bishop.

It was not long in coming. The next morning, the Bishop set out with a small retinue to visit various parts of his diocese. On the way, they were surrounded by a strong force of men-at-arms led by Stephen le Poer, the Seneschal's brother. With drawn swords, they escorted the Bishop as a prisoner to Kilkenny castle.

The Bishop's immediate reaction was to place the entire diocese under a religious interdict, which meant that every inhabitant

RIGHT
Fanciful view of sorcery – a
beautiful witch arises as a sorcerer
chants incantations from an occult
book, the Compendium
Maleficorum.

stood in peril of being refused the sacraments and perhaps excommunicated. It was a crafty form of religious blackmail designed to sway the masses over to his side – but the Seneschal immediately parried this move by calling upon anyone who had a complaint to make against the Bishop of Ossary to lay it before the authorities at once. Not a soul came forward.

Many people bore a grudge against the Bishop, and he was indirectly accused of a number of crimes, but no-one dared to bring outright charges against him. In the end the Seneschal, realizing that public opinion was turning against him, was forced to release the prelate after holding him for 18 days.

Just how he managed it is unfortunately not recorded, but the Bishop of Ossary eventually did succeed in obtaining permission to bring the alleged sorcerers to trial. But Lady Alice was not one of them; she was taken secretly to England together with Sarah de Meath, and although the true facts are not known she is said to have ended her days there in peace. Her accomplices were all found guilty on lesser charges and were sentenced to be publicly whipped, after which they were released.

There were two exceptions, William Outlawe and Petronella de Meath. Poor Petronella was made the scapegoat for the absent Lady Alice; she was horribly tortured, and between her screams of agony a 'confession' was extracted from her. She was whipped six times through the streets of Kilkenny, then burned at the stake in front of a large crowd. Her confession, it was alleged, included a statement to the effect that she herself had considerable powers as a witch, but that compared with Lady Alice she was a novice. Her mistress had taught her all she knew, and she believed there was no more powerful witch in the world.

William Outlawe duly appeared before the ecclesiastical court in Kilkenny – armed to the teeth and surrounded by equally heavily-armed supporters. He was found guilty, but no-one dared arrest him. He simply walked out of the courtroom, as good as free. His eventual fate is unknown, but he left Kilkenny and it is thought that he may have entered the service of one of the country's powerful barons.

As far as Seneschal Arnald le Poer was concerned, the Bishop certainly had the last word. Accused and found guilty of heresy, the unfortunate Arnald was excommunicated and flung into the dungeons of Dublin Castle. He was still there 10 years later, when Roger Outlawe – who had meanwhile climbed the ranks to become Lord Justice of Ireland – attempted to intercede on his behalf. The Bishop of Ossary promptly accused Roger himself of heresy, and the attempt to save the former Seneschal was hurriedly abandoned. Not that it mattered, because le Poer conveniently died in the meantime.

However, the Bishop's tactics proved to be double-edged, for allegations of heresy were made against him too in due course. With a long history of unpopularity and alleged crimes behind him, he saw the writing on the wall and fled to Italy.

The Kyteler case is important for two reasons. First of all, it was the first witch-trial in Ireland – and poor Petronella de Meath had the dubious distinction of being the first witch to be burned in that country. But apart from that, the details of the trial – the sacrifices at the crossroads, the flying on brooms, the copulation with demons, the preparation of nauseating potions for evil purposes, the weird incantations – it was all to be repeated so many times, in almost identical detail, in witch-trials between the fourteenth and eighteenth centuries.

But many people believe that the most fascinating figure in the whole case was not Lady Alice, but the demon known as Robert Artisson. Just who or what he was will never be known, but he was clearly the leader of the coven, and made up the required number of 13. It is possible that his true identity was unknown to the witches, since it was not revealed in the tortured ravings of Petronella. One theory suggests that he was simply a peasant from a neighbouring district, with little more attribute than considerable sexual prowess; but he must have been extremely quick-witted and resourceful to evade the net cast wide by the Bishop of Ossary.

Or perhaps he was a supernatural being after all. Perhaps, under different guises, he went on appearing at Satanic rituals long after Lady Alice and her accomplices were dead. Perhaps, like Pandora, it was Lady Alice who turned the key that let loose on man one more evil spirit.

ABOVE

This coloured engraving from 1555 (and thus roughly contemporary with the Kyteler case), shows witches being burnt at the stake in Germany – this barbarous treatment was meted out all over medieval Europe.

BELOW
Frans Francken's magnificent
painting of a witches' sabbath, in
the Victoria and Albert Museum,
London.

CHAPTER 7

The Children of the Damned

The twin villages of Mora and Elfdale lay in the heart of some of the most beautiful country in the world: the mountains and lakes of central Sweden. There was peace here, as well as beauty. The villagers, nurtured by the crisp air that brought a sweet tang of pines with it as it swept down from the mist-covered slopes above the lakes, were robust and carefree. Simple people, few of them were deeply religious in an orthodox manner; yet in their own way, because of the peace and beauty that was their heritage, they were close to the heart of God.

But that was before the Devil kidnapped their children.

It happened quite suddenly. A child grew pale and listless. That night, when he fell asleep, his terrified parents thought that he was dead. His body was unnaturally cold and rigid. In fact, the child was in what would nowadays be called a cataleptic trance. As he emerged from it, he began to moan and thrash about as though in a paroxysm of terror. When he awoke, he was a different person. His eyes had a faraway, ecstatic look; it was as if he were in the middle of a waking dream. A degree of normality returned as the day wore on – but as soon as darkness fell the child lapsed into his uncanny trance once more.

LEFT
The village church of Mora. The local community was deeply religious in a simple way.

FACING PAGE
It was rumoured that the children of Mora and Elfdale were being abducted and forced to take part in Satanic ceremonies.

First one child, then 10, 20, 50 even 100 were affected in a similar way. A strange, terrifying rumour began to circulate. The children, it was whispered, were being abducted by witches and forced to take part in satanic ceremonies, after which they were allowed to go home again. It was said that the pastor of Elfdale had written a letter to his bishop in which he claimed to have conclusive proof that an eight-year-old girl had been initiated into a witches' coven by a 17-year-old servant girl. An old crone of 70 had also confessed to abducting children and using the innocent bodies for all manner of vile perversions.

Thoroughly alarmed, several of the leading citizens of Mora and Elfdale drafted a petition to the King of Sweden, Charles XI. At that time – it was 1668 – the monarch himself was only 14 years old, and his decisions were made for him by his State Council. The Council – mindful of the fact that the rest of Europe was in the grip of witchcraft fever and anxious to avoid similar scandals in Sweden – decided that the villagers' petition merited an investigation. They appointed two commissioners, gave them the power to interrogate witnesses and to take whatever action might be necessary to put an end to any mischief, and sent them to Elfdale to find out exactly what was going on.

BELOW
Dark and brooding lakeland in southern Sweden. Most Satanic rites were held by water.

FACING PAGE
The children said that the Devil used to appear, and provide them with strange, unearthly animals on which to ride.

It was the start of one of history's strangest and most sinister witch trials, a trial that led to the persecution of innocent children while the real culprits, whoever they were, went free.

The chief witnesses were the parents of the 100 children who were said to have been carried away by the witches. But it was the children themselves who provided the sensational details of the horror they had experienced. In small, stupefied voices, they told how they had been carried away to a place called Blakolla, although they had no idea where this was. There, they had taken part in mysterious rites and orgies, culminating in a feast presided over by a devil whom they called Locyta.

A deathly silence fell over the assembly – 3,000 strong – as the commissioners asked the children to tell exactly how they had reached this mysterious place called Blakolla. The tale they told was incredible, and all the more horrifying for the fact that each child told it in perfect detail, their faces expressionless masks, as though they were reciting a well-known nursery rhyme.

The children said that first of all they had gone to a gravel-pit that lay near a crossroads. There, they had draped cloths over their heads and danced around blindly until they were almost exhausted. The dance over, they then ran to the crossroads, where they formed a circle. Three times – softly at first, then louder, then very loud – they cried the ritual summons:

'Antecessor, come and carry us to Blakolla!'

Then, they said, the 'devil' used to appear. They described him as a big man, with a bushy red beard, who wore colourful red or blue clothes. They told the shocked assembly that the man had been kindly – not at all like the foul fiend the Devil was supposed to be – and that he had laughed a lot. The children had not been in the least afraid of him.

The devil provided them with strange, unearthly animals for the ride to Blakolla. He also gave them witches' ointment, which had the power to make them fly through the air on broomsticks.

The Black Sabbat was held in a big house that stood alone in a meadow. There, the children were made to swear allegiance to Satan. They had to devote themselves to him, body and soul, and were given satanic names. They were also threatened that if they revealed any of the cult's secrets, they would be slowly tortured and beaten to death.

At their initiation ceremony, which was held by the side of a lake, each child was given a bag filled with metal filings taken from a church bell. The bag was then thrown into the water, with the words: 'As these filings from the bell can never return to the bell, so may my soul never return to heaven.'

After the ceremony, the initiates sat down to a feast, the favourites sitting next to the 'devil'. Sometimes the food was excellent; sometimes it was nauseating, a concoction of foul ingredients which the children were forced to eat.

Then there was dancing. While the 'devil' played a harp, the children were made to dance half naked in front of him. Sometimes, they were beaten by the coven's 'priests' out of sheer sadism, and sexual perversions were also practised. In fact, the whole conduct of the coven was closely parallel to that of covens in England and elsewhere in Europe.

The children were also taught how to cast harmful spells. They confessed that on one occasion they had put a spell on the pastor of Elfdale by hammering a nail into the head of a wooden effigy; the pastor confirmed that he had been experiencing unusually severe headaches for the first time in his life.

That was the chidren's story. Fantastic though it appeared to the commissioners, one fact above all others made it seem credible – each child told a tale that was identical, down to the most minute detail, with that of his fellows. Seventy adults were also

WELCOME TO HELL

The spirits of the Norse lands are grim creations, and become more so the farther north one travels. In Finland, only certain evil spirits can pass the Loathsome River and Surma, the guardian monster that lurks on the opposite bank, to reach Tuonela, the Land of the Dead. This is ruled by Tuoni and his wife Tuonetar, who are helped by their daughters Kipu-Tytto, the spirit of sickness, and Loviatar, the spirit of all evil, with her plague-ravaged face and nine children who bear the names of the diseases that were the scourge of medieval times. Tuonetar welcomes newcomers to hell with a mug of ale filled with frogs and worms.

accused of being implicated in some way with the satanic rituals; 23 of them confessed to the crime of witchcraft and were subsequently beheaded, their bodies afterwards being burned.

One thing above all puzzled the interrogators. Although the children swore that they had actually been present in the flesh at the Sabbat, many of their parents were adamant that the young ones had never left the house. Then one of the accused – a girl – admitted that there had been occasions when the devil had only taken away her spirit, leaving her body behind. Still utterly perplexed, the commissioners accepted the statement. They had all the evidence they wanted; most of the accused had confessed, and all that remained for them to do now was to pass sentence.

It was a harsh one. Fifteen of the children, between the ages of nine and 16, were executed. Sixty more were sentenced to be birched, and to be caned severely once a week for a year. No

attempt was made to locate Blakolla, or to trace the mysterious high priest known as Locyta – the 'devil' of the children's story. To the superstitious people, the story alone was proof enough that the children had been in the hands of supernatural forces. There was little point in searching for a phantom.

It was a pity, for if Locyta and the place where the Sabbat was held had been identified, some interesting facts might have been unearthed. And there can be little doubt that Locyta would have proved just as vulnerable as the innocent children he had led astray, and who had shed their blood because of him.

Today, experts who have studied the strange case of the 'be-witched' children of Elfdale and Mora believe that the children were the victims of either mass hypnosis or some form of drug – perhaps a primitive version of LSD, manufactured from certain fungi. Many of the experiences they claimed to have undergone – such as flying through the air – could in fact have been pure hallucination. But there was one major snag: no two hallucinations would have been alike, and the children's accounts were absolutely identical in every respect.

During the trial, the interrogators had completely overlooked one aspect that linked the whole affair closely with the accepted pattern of European witchcraft: the phenomenon known as the 'dreaming soul'. Many witches in their confessions, had admitted that they sometimes confused dreams with reality. One writer, Sinistrari, said in his *Demoniality*, published in 1700:

> 'There is no question that sometimes young women, de-
> ceived by the Demon, imagine that they are actually taking
> part in the Sabbats of witches, and all this is merest fantasy.
> But this is not always the case; on the contrary, it more
> often happens that witches are bodily present at Sabbats and
> have an actual carnal and corporeal connection with the
> Demon.'

Some inquisitors believed that the Devil had no power to trans-port a witch's body away, and that the Sabbats were held in the spirit while the witch's material body was sleeping. She was said to lie down on her left side and place herself in a trance, whereupon her spirit crept out of her mouth in the form of a bluish vapour.

All this, however, supposes that the witch is already an initiate and has been endowed with mystical powers. The same could not be said of the Swedish children. They were the victims of some overwhelming external force. The question is, what force?

Suppose a small band of people, far advanced on the occult path, led by a black magician possessing immense powers – powers that included the ability to set up some form of telepathic com-munication with the untroubled mind of a sleeping child. And not just one child, but 100. Subconciously the children receive an order

to go to a certain place at a certain time. The next day, the children rendezvous at the gravel-pit near the crossroads. The magician appears and leads them to the Sabbat like a kind of satanic pied piper. Afterwards, the children are ordered to forget the place and the way to it; their memory of the journey is hypnotically supplanted by a surrealist dream. And the next night, as the children sleep, they enter a trance-like state as the telepathic command comes to them again.

Fantastic? Maybe. But today, we know that such abominations are at least theoretically possible – and fact is often far, far stranger than fiction.

As to who Locyta really was, that we shall never know, nor what his purpose was; whether it was an attempt to form a 'new order' of satanists, or merely a means of satisfying his own perverted lust, is doomed to remain a mystery. The adults who were brought to trial were mere puppets; they knew as little about the mysterious magician as did the children. Locyta and his acolytes vanished from the face of the earth.

But old legends and superstitions die hard. Even today, more than 300 years later, the memory is still strong in that part of Sweden of the time when the children of two villages were possessed by dark forces.

ABOVE
Seventeenth-century representation of a witches' sabbath, perhaps based on a scene from a play.

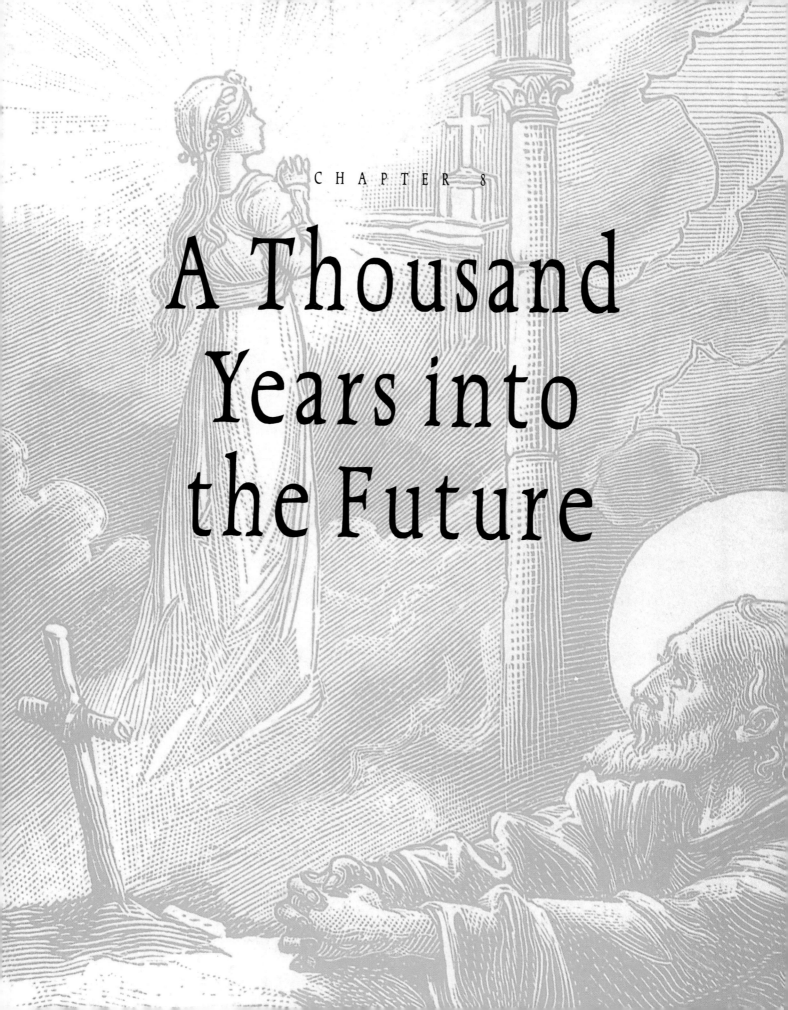

CHAPTER 8

A Thousand Years into the Future

I n 1 April, 1945, armoured units of the First French Army smashed their way across the Rhine into southern Germany. En route, they thundered through the cobbled streets of a picturesque mountain village called Odelianburg. As the tanks roared past a little tree-lined churchyard, the crews traversed their machine-guns vigilantly, for the trees and the gravestones might be sheltering snipers. But the Shermans clattered on without incident, the men inside them completely unaware that in that churchyard was the tomb of an amazing woman – one who, more than 1,000 years earlier, had foretold the coming of the armoured monsters.

Her name was Saint Odelia. She was born in 660, the daughter of Adalric, the Duke of Alsace. Legend tells us that she was blind from birth, but that when she became a Christian at the age of 59, she miraculously received her sight. An obscure saint whose day is celebrated on 13 December, she is remembered for two things. The first is a monastery in the Vosges Mountains, which she had built; the second is an incredible flash of prophecy which came to her as she was writing a letter to her brother.

It is only now that we can realize the full extent of that amazing prophecy – for in her letter of 12 centuries ago, St Odelia described the events of the Second World War with uncanny accuracy.

LEFT
April, 1945. American troops cross into southern Germany. The event was foretold over 1,000 years earlier by St Odelia.

ABOVE
Adolf Hitler – the 'antichrist' who
arose from the banks of the River
Danube to bring war and famine to
the world.

'My brother,' she wrote in Latin, 'my heart is filled with fear, for I have seen the horror that will overwhelm the forests and the mountains. When that time comes, men will curse the name of Germany and call her the most warlike nation in the world. From her belly she will spawn a terrible warrior who will be called the Antichrist. War and famine he will spread across the world, and his name will be a curse on the lips of thousands of mothers, the blood of whose children will redden his sword and whose homes he shall bring down in destruction.

'The warrior shall bring such agony to the world as man has never seen. From the banks of the Danube he will come, and shall stand out as a great chief among men.'

There can be no doubt that this part of the prophecy refers to Hitler. He was born within sight of the Danube, his lust for power plunged the world into the most frightful war in history, he was hated and cursed by millions, not thousands of people – and no-one will argue with the fact that in an evil way he was a leader of considerable talent.

'His soldiers,' St Odelia goes on, 'will bear weapons of fire. They will set the world aflame, and on their helmets shall blaze the flash of the thunder- bolt.' The insignia of Hitler's SS regiments was a double lightning flash. 'Red will be the hands of the conquerors,' she continued. 'Unbelievable cruelty and torture will they inflict upon the unhappy world.'

Ten million souls died in Hitler's extermination camps, and all over Europe, villages were razed to the ground as reprisals against resistance and their inhabitants murdered.

'Everywhere shall his legions be victorious. In their winged chariots they shall mount to the very vault of heaven, to seize the stars and hurl them to the earth in a blaze of fire. The earth will

THE CIRCLE OF TIME?

Sometimes, individuals can recall the events of past centuries with great clarity, a phenomenon that has given rise to theories of reincarnation. One possible explanation is that there are timeless cells locked within our brains, passed from generation to generation, that form an ongoing record of our ancestry. But can people really foretell future events? That is quite a different matter, and one that may be linked with the nature of time itself. If the future is completely determined by present events, then in some sense the future is already contained in the present. Time, like all else in the universe, may be a circle; it was represented in ancient times by a snake with its tail in its mouth. If various points of the circle can be intercepted by occult means, then it might be possible to visualize both past and future events.

tremble, the rivers run red with blood. From the depths of the oceans dark sea-monsters shall rise to maim and destroy. His enemies will be powerful, but they will reel before him. Only one will not fall, but shall gather her strength and throw up a mighty bulwark to stem the conqueror's tide.'

First, the *Anschluss* joined Austria to Germany. Then Czechoslovakia was overrun, followed by Poland, Norway, Denmark, France, Holland and Belgium all came under the jackboot, until at the end of 1940 Great Britain stood alone against the might of Nazi Germany.

'At last, in the sixth month of the war's second year, the conqueror's star will begin to wane. He shall call down misfortune upon the heads of his enemies, yet they will not submit.'

The Second World War began in 1939, so the date prophesied by St Odelia would coincide with June, 1941 – the month in which Hitler launched his great offensive against Russia, a decision which was destined to turn the tide of war against him.

St Odelia predicted that there would subsequently follow a long period of attrition. 'Twenty nations will be locked in a bitter

BELOW
'Only one will not fall . . .' In 1940, Britain stood alone in defiance of Nazism. Here, RAF fighter pilots relax between missions in the Battle of Britain.

LEFT
German tanks advance into Russia in the winter of 1941. The invasion of Russia marked the beginning of the end for Hitler's ambitions.

struggle for supremacy. New terrors from the skies cause the earth to tremble, and men will cry out for peace, but their cries will fall on deaf ears.'

The new terrors from the skies could refer to the jet aircraft and rocket weapons which Hitler's scientists developed for operational use in 1944. In the second half of that year, London and Antwerp were subjected to a fearful blitz by the V-1 and V-2 missiles. In that year, a group of Germans also tried to assassinate Hitler. On every front, Germany was fighting desperately to hold on to the vast territories she had overrun.

'Then, like an avalanche, the last days shall come. The earth of the conqueror's homeland shall tremble under the iron-shod feet of his enemies. His kingdom shall be plunged into blood and darkness. For the memory of his cruelty and injustice will be strong in the minds of men, and they shall show no mercy. By his own hand shall the conqueror perish, bereft of his legions and deserted by his counsellors.' On 30 April, 1945, Adolf Hitler – with the thunder of Russian guns in his ears and Berlin in flames around him – committed suicide.

'But in the East,' warns St Odelia, 'the fury of war is not yet spent. The distant legions of the conqueror fight on for a space, until at last they are afflicted by an unknown and terrible disease.' Long after the rubble of Hiroshima and Nagasaki had been cleared

away, thousands of people in Japan were still falling victim to an 'unknown and terrible illness' – radiation sickness. Was this what St Odelia saw in her vision?

Or did she really 'see' anything at all?

The letters which she wrote to her brother, the Duke of Franconia, have long since been lost. The earliest reference to them, and their content, comes from an eleventh-century monastic source. No reference is made to them in the approved biographies of the saints, other than the occasional mention that the story of Saint Odelia is surrounded by 'remarkable legends'.

But the letters, and the prophecies contained in them, are not a modern invention. Hundreds of years ago, *someone* – and there is no reason to doubt that it was St Odelia – was given a strange power to penetrate the mists of the future with a far greater clarity and accuracy than the ambiguous ramblings of more acceptable prophets such as Nostradamus.

The prophecy of St Odelia ends with a glimpse of the nuclear terror that crushed Japan. If she saw any further than that, there is no record of it. Perhaps it is just as well.

The early centuries of the Christian Church spawned a great many prophets, but few of them are as well documented as Mael Maedoc ua Morgair, better known by his scriptural name of Malachi. An Irish monk, born in 1095, he eventually became Archbishop of Armagh and was a close friend of St Bernard of Clairvaux.

In 1595, 500 years after Malachi was born, a Dominican friar named Arnold de Wion published a book of prophecies that were said to be the work of the Irish monk. De Wion claimed that they had been written by Malachi during a visit to Rome in his later years, and after having been read and approved by Pope Innocent II, the manuscript had been placed in the Vatican archives, where it had lain undisturbed for five centuries.

The prophecies consisted of 111 brief Latin mottoes, which purported to identify each successive pope from Celestine II, of Malachi's time, to what was described as 'the time of the end'.

One of the first popes dealt with by the prophecy after the manuscript was published was Leo XI, who was described as 'Waveman; like the wind he came, and like the water he went.' Leo reigned for only 27 days, and in 1605 was succeeded by Paul V, whose prophetic motto was 'Perverse people'. His reign was characterized by difficulties with the rapidly-growing Protestant population of Europe, which made the motto fit. Malachi was even more accurate with Pope Alexander VII, who reigned from 1655 to 1667, and whose motto was 'Guardian of the Hills'. Alexander's family arms in fact portrayed three hills, watched over by a star.

One prophecy in particular catches the imagination. It concerns Pope Clement X, whose reign lasted only six years, from 1670 to

FACING PAGE
The ruins of Nagasaki, which along with Hiroshima was devastated by atomic bombs in August 1945. Was this what St Odelia foresaw?

FACING PAGE
Malachi, the twelfth-century Irish monk who was also said to be gifted with prophecy, mainly concerning the popes.

RIGHT
Pope Gregory XVI, who came from a religious order in Etruria that specialized in archaeological research.

1676. According to Malachi, the identifying motto was 'Concerning the Mighty River'. When Clement was a baby, the river Tiber overflowed its banks and poured into his home, almost sweeping him away. He would have drowned if his nurse had not caught hold of him at the last instant. Apart from that, his family coat of arms depicted the Milky Way – and in Latin, the term for Milky Way was Magnum Flumen, or Great River.

The motto of Pope Innocent XIII (1721–4) was 'Of Good Religion', and there was no denying the fact that this pope came from an extremely religious family. His successor, Benedict XIII (1724–32), was just the opposite; his family had produced nothing but soldiers for generations, and his motto was 'Soldier in Battle'.

To the 94th pope on the list, Malachi gave the motto 'Rose of Umbria'; Clement XIII, whose motto it was, lived in Umbria before he became pope, and Umbria's symbol was a rose. Clement XIV's (1769–75) coat of arms incorporated the symbol of a running bear – and once again Malachi was extraordinarily accurate with his motto 'Swift Bear'.

The same was true of Gregory XVI (1831–46), of whom Malachi wrote 'Concerning the Baths of Etruria'. It was a strange motto – but Gregory XVI did in fact come from a religious order in Etruria that specialized in archaeological research, particularly in connection with the 'balnea', or ancient baths, for which the province was famous.

Pope Leo XIII, who reigned from 1878 to 1903, took the prophecies into the twentieth century. His motto was 'Light in the Sky', and his crest was a comet on an azure field.

About this time, there was a good deal of speculation – not to say apprehension – in religious circles about the motto connected with the 104th pope. The motto was 'Religion Depopulated'. The motto seemed to have a sinister ring to it, and it came strangely true, for the 104th pope, Benedict XV, was chosen in 1914, the year that saw the outbreak of the First World War, resulting in the deaths of millions of people – mostly Christians – on the battlefields of Europe. Then, in 1917, came the Russian Revolution – and

LEFT	ABOVE
Lenin addressing his followers during the October Revolution. Thousands turned their backs on Christianity in the years that followed.	*After 1941, volunteers from many countries (including neutral Spain), responded to Hitler's call to attack the USSR and Communism – an event foretold by Malachi.*

under the new Soviet regime millions more people turned their backs on Christianity and found a new 'religion' in Communism. The struggle against Communism characterized the reign of Benedict's successor, Pius XI (1922–39); he fought against the Communist purges against the Catholic Church in Russia and Spain, and his motto was 'Intrepid Faith'.

'Angelic Pastor' was how Malachi described Pope Pius XII (1939–58) – and this too seemed to fit well, because Pius was regarded as a saint even by many non-Catholics. The motto for Pope John XXIII (1958–63), however, was baffling; he was described as 'Pastor and Sailor'. But a sailor he was not – unless the motto referred to his pilgrimages abroad.

But the most sinister prophetic motto of all concerns the present-day Pope, John Paul II, who was elected in 1978. It is 'Concerning the Cresent Moon'. The crescent moon is the symbol of Islam, and it is the Islamic Revolution that today presents the greatest threat to Christianity since the Middle Ages.

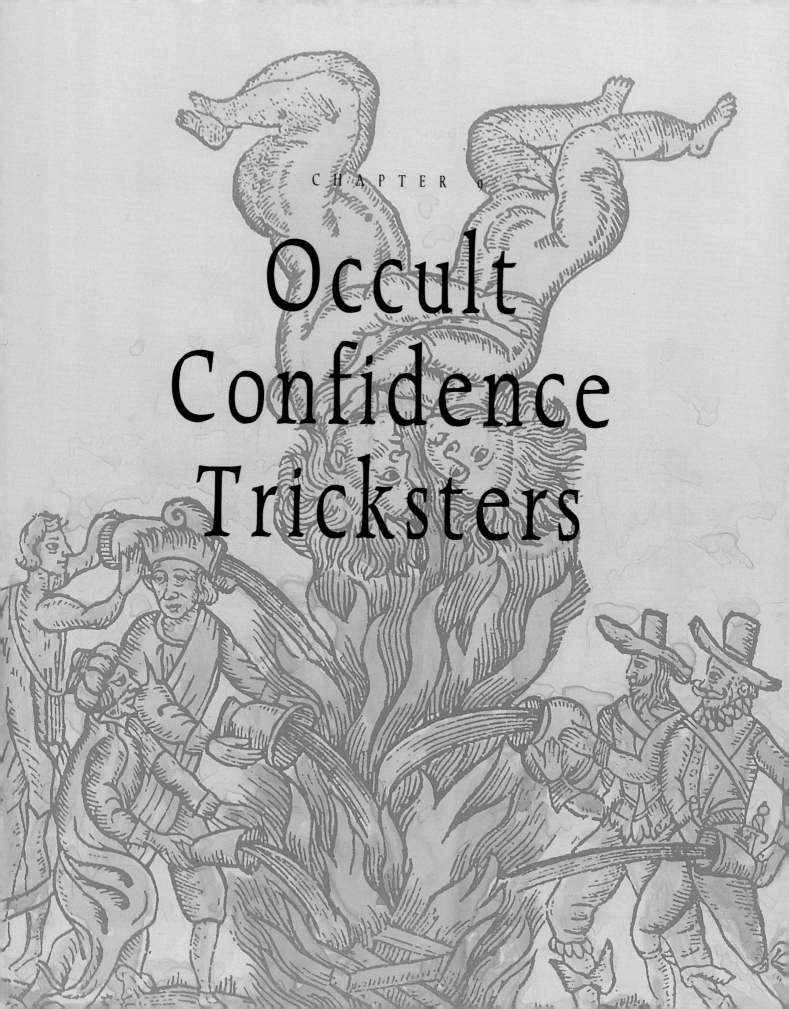

CHAPTER 9

Occult
Confidence
Tricksters

On a low cliff overlooking England's River Nidd, close to the picturesque North Yorkshire market town of Knaresborough, there is a cave. An iron grille at its entrance protects what is inside: an effigy of a witch, complete with hooked nose and conical hat, and one of her black cat. The cave also contains other traditional trappings of witchery, such as a broomstick and a cauldron. The place is called Mother Shipton's Cave.

The folk who lived in and around Knaresborough during the early years of the sixteenth century knew her and feared her. They said she was a witch; she lived the life of a hermit and it was rumoured that she had sold her soul to the Devil. Small children, threatened by cross parents with the possibility that she might come at dead of night and carry them off if they didn't stop being naughty, had nightmares about her bulbous, warty nose and her small, glittering eyes.

Nevertheless, no-one would deny that Mother Ursula Shipton had her uses. She had an incredibly wide knowledge of herbal

FACING PAGE
The Great Plague. A maniac, a celebrated figure in London at the time, prophesied the city's doom.

BELOW
Mother Ursula Shipton supposedly casting a horoscope for a client. From a sixteenth-century pamphlet.

remedies. For a modest fee she would make a potion that would cure a sick cow or make hens lay, and frequent visitors to her cave included women who wanted aphrodisiacs – or abortions. Her prowess undoubtedly saved her life. Anyone else would probably have been drowned or burned to death by witch-hunters.

Few of Mother Shipton's clients, however, could have dreamed that this foul old crone would be remembered even when they had been dust for more than four centuries. Remembered not because of her remedies, but because she was alleged to have made a number of strange and disturbing prophecies – predictions which were ridiculed at the time, but which have come true, one by one, over the centuries.

Among other things, she was supposed to have predicted the defeat of the Spanish Armada in 1588; the downfall and death of Cardinal Wolsey in the time of Henry VIII; the discovery of vast goldfields in Australia, long before anyone dreamed that there was such a place as Australia; the Great Fire of London; and the plague that ravaged England in the seventeenth century.

Over the years, researchers kept turning up new predictions. Some of them were concerned with terrible wars that would occur in the twentieth century, and with the progress of science – including the invention of air travel, submarines, automobiles and wireless. Many of these were subsequently found to be elaborate forgeries, made during the nineteenth century – but even so, the forgeries appeared in print long before the advent of the things they predicted.

Towards the middle of the nineteenth century, a pamphlet appeared in England containing some 'newly-discovered Mother Shipton prophecies'. Two in particular caused a sensation. The first told of terrible things to come in the twentieth century:

> 'In nineteen hundred and thirty-six
> Build houses light with straw and sticks
> For then shall mighty wars be planned
> And fire and sword shall sweep the land.
> But those who live the century through
> In fear and trembling this shall do.
> Fleet to the mountains and the dens
> To bogs and forest and wild fens
> For storms shall rage and oceans roar
> When Gabriel stands on sea and shore
> And as he blows his wondrous horn
> Old worlds shall die and new be born.'

ABOVE
Mother Shipton is credited with predicting the defeat of the Spanish Armada in 1588 – the same year in which Nicholas Hilliard painted this magnificent epic battle scene.

And the second dealt with scientific marvels to come:

'Carriages without horses shall go
And accidents fill the world with woe.
Around the earth thoughts shall fly
In the twinkling of an eye.
Through the hills man shall ride
And no horse shall be at his side.
Under water men shall walk
Shall ride, shall sleep, shall talk.
In the air men shall be seen
In white and black and green.
Iron in the water shall float
As easily as a wooden boat.'

A few years later, the credulous public realized it had been taken for a ride, for the real author of these prophecies turned out to be an English editor named Charles Hindley, who had been having a good laugh at everyone's expense.

It had not been difficult for him to arrive at the scientific conclusions outlined in the 'prophecy'; prototypes of ironclad ships and crude submarines had already been built when he wrote it, and balloons were fast becoming commonplace. A good deal of imagination, plus intelligent guesswork, had enabled him to predict the probable course of scientific events.

The prediction concerning the year 1936 was a little more puzzling. Hindley could not possibly have known that this year would see the outbreak of the bloody Spanish Civil War, and its dreadful aftermath of World War Two; nor could he have foreseen that many of the world's inhabitants during the latter half of the twentieth century would indeed live 'in fear and trembling' at the prospect of a nuclear holocaust. There is one possible solution that might account for his uncanny accuracy, and it is that Hindley might have been a clairvoyant in his own right. Unfortunately, we shall never know.

After the revelation that these sensational prophecies were fakes, there was a natural tendency to dismiss all predictions attributed to Mother Shipton as forgeries. In fact, it was not until 1641, 80 years after her reputed death in 1561, that the first of her prophecies came to light.

The most famous prediction of all was that concerning the fate of Cardinal Wolsey. When Wolsey was at the summit of his political career as England's Prime Minister, he was summoned by Henry VIII to meet the king in York. Mother Shipton, so the story goes, predicted that it was an appointment he would never keep. Wolsey heard of this, and in anger he sent a party of men to force the old woman to withdraw her statement. Blandly, she told them that they would share the fate of their master; she was so convincing that they left her unharmed and went away in fear of what was going to happen to them.

Wolsey never did keep that appointment. Henry, angered by the Cardinal's failure to persuade Pope Clement to annul the marriage bet-ween him and Catherine of Aragon, had him seized and charged with treason. He died a few months later, in Leicester, on his way to stand trial in London.

One of the men who had visited Mother Shipton at the Cardinal's command was Thomas Cromwell, the Earl of Essex and Wolsey's legal secretary. Ten years later, after succeeding the Cardinal as First Minister, he was also arrested and charged with treason. He was beheaded in 1540, which must have brought a cackle of glee from Mother Shipton when she heard the news.

ABOVE
Charles Hindley could not have envisaged the Spanish Civil War, whose outbreak he predicted accurately. Picture shows a poster issued by the General Union of Workers in Spain, 1938.

FACING PAGE
King Henry VIII, seen here in a painting at Windsor Castle, also featured in Shipton's prophecies.

A second batch of predictions was published in 1667. The long delay was explained by the story that they had been held in trust by a woman named Joanne Waller, whom Mother Shipton had befriended when she was a small child. The prophetess had made Joanne promise never to reveal the predictions while she, Joanne, still lived. Now Joanne had died at the age of 94, and the prophecies could at last be released.

The predictions dealt with the death of Henry VIII, the reign of Queen Elizabeth I, the decline of Roman Catholicism in Britain, the defeat of the Spanish Armada and the execution of Mary, Queen of Scots. If the predictions really were made by Mother Shipton during her lifetime, they were amazingly accurate. They also included a vision which was taken to refer to the Great Fire of London; in it Mother Shipton visualized a boat sailing up the Thames, the crew gazing in horror and astonishment at the desolation that had replaced all the familiar buildings. Finally, there was a vague prophecy that was intriguing because it could refer to a war that has been – or a war that is yet to come. It reads:

BOTTOM LEFT
The Spanish Armada, here setting sail for England, was defeated by Queen Elizabeth I's sailors.

BELOW
Queen Elizabeth I engineered the execution of Mary, Queen of Scots, foretold by Mother Shipton.

'Then shall come the Son of Man, having a fierce beast in his arms, whose kingdom lies in the Land of the Moon, which is dreadful throughout the whole world; with a number of people he shall pass many waters and come to the Land of the Lion. Look for help of the beast of his country, and an eagle shall come out of the East, spread with the beams of the Son of Man, and shall destroy the castles of the Thames, and there shall be a battle among many kingdoms.

'And therewith shall be crowned the Son of Man, and the fourth year shall be many battles for the faith and the Son of Man, when the eagles shall be preferred, and there shall be peace over the world, and there shall be plenty of fruit, and then shall he go to the Land of the Cross.'

The eagles 'coming from the East' to 'destroy the castles of the Thames' could be construed as referring to the air-raids on Britain during the Second World War. On the other hand, the prophecy strongly resembles a strange mixture of the Book of Revelation and the prophecies of Nostradamus. The latter also referred to the

LONDONS *fier began September the second,* 1666.

o be fold by Tho: Parkhurft Nath: Ranew and Jonath: Robinfon

A WORD FOR THE WISE

Mother Shipton was a benevolent witch – if, indeed, she was a witch at all – and typical of many country women of her era, who had the ability to administer simple herbal remedies, forecast the weather accurately, and give wholesome advice to their neighbours. There is no evidence that such so-called 'witches' ever did harm to anyone. The modern notion that a witch was always a hideous, spiteful old hag is quite ridiculous, and takes no account of the fact that there were almost as many male witches as female. Before the terrible persecutions of the seventeenth century, witches often sat on the councils of kings and took an active part in the affairs of state. Male witches involved in such activities sometimes wore a distinguishing uniform – as did the viziers of the Orient – and females, at an earlier date, wore robes decked with black lambskin and white catskin, studded with gems.

97

Land of the Moon, meaning the home of the Muslims – the biggest threat to Christianity then, as indeed they are now.

In fact, close examination reveals not one shred of proof to show that Mother Shipton actually made any of these prophecies. All that has survived is the legend that was built up around her long after her death – a legend that has long since stifled any small spark of truth. So are these a host of useless prophecies written by charlatans through four successive centuries? Or is this intelligent guess closer to the truth. Perhaps Mother Ursula Shipton was a harmless, if repugnant, old woman who earned a reputation for herself by brewing potions and by making a few minor predictions – about the weather, about livestock, and about people in her area – predictions based on shrewd reasoning and even shrewder powers of observation.

After her death, the legend that surrounds her probably originated, like so many other legends, in yarns swapped over a tankard of ale. And all it needs for a legend to grow and become embroidered is the passage of years.

BELOW
Another legend, similar to the Shipton one, surrounds St Ninian's well near Carlisle. It claimed that anyone who drank from the waters would have the gift of second sight.

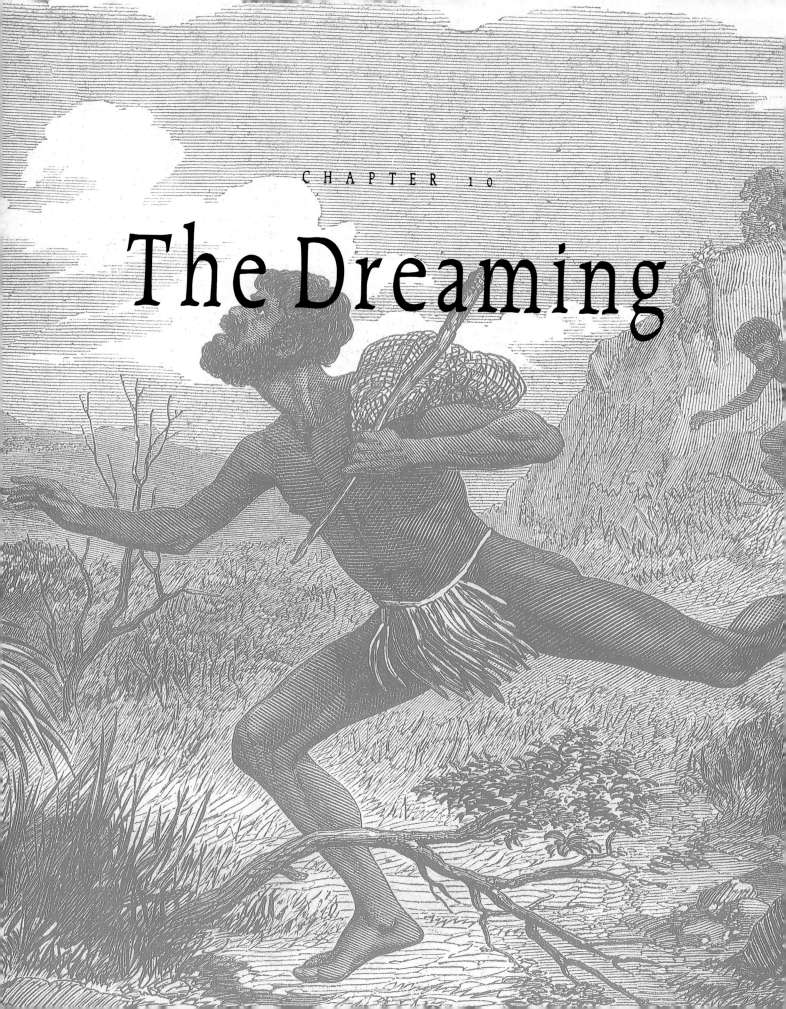

CHAPTER 10

The Dreaming

The aborigines of Australia call it the Dreaming, or the Dreamtime. It represents the birth of the world, and from it came the gods that still stalk the tribal lands of the southern continent today. Many of the gods took human form, and gave the aborigines their secrets – secrets of ritual and magic that no 'civilized' mind can comprehend. Secrets of The Dreaming . . .

In April 1943, Australia was threatened with invasion by the Japanese. Enemy forces were massing in New Guinea and had occupied most of the strategic points on the island except the area around Port Moresby on the south-eastern tip, a comparative stone's throw away from the Australian mainland.

For a year, Japanese bombers based on the island of Timor had been carrying out frequent attacks on Darwin, the vital Australian port through which supplies were being channelled to New Guinea in readiness for the decisive battle that was soon to come. To defend the Darwin area, there were a few squadrons of the Royal Australian Air Force, the Royal Air Force – which had sent

LEFT
P-40 Tomahawk fighters warm up
before a mission against the enemy,
Northern Australia, 1942.

BELOW
Australian aboriginal medicine man
with magic body markings, from a
photograph c1900.

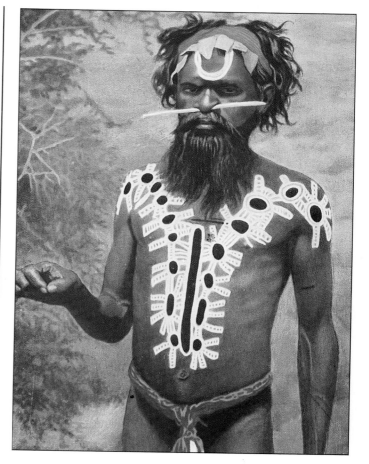

Spitfires out from Britain – and the 49th Fighter Group of the United States Army Air Force, which flew P-40 Warhawk fighters.

One of the 49th's pilots was Lieutenant Pete Johnston, who took off that April on a mission to intercept a force of Japanese raiders. Intent on destroying a twin-engined enemy bomber, he failed to see the Jap 'Zero' fighter that crept up on his tail until it was too late. The first he knew of the enemy fighter's presence was when cannon shells smashed into his P-40 and the world blew up in his face.

As his cripped fighter spun down out of control, Johnston managed to throw back the cockpit canopy and bale out. Hanging in his harness under the billowing parachute canopy, he looked around. The fight had taken him miles to the south-west of Darwin, and he had no idea of his exact position. Minutes later, Johnston thudded to earth in the midst of a mangrove swamp.

It was the beginning of a six-day ordeal, a ceaseless struggle against stinking, clinging mud; against crocodiles, snakes, and a thousand varieties of poisonous insects. It was a living nightmare that would inevitably have ended in a fearful death, his bones lying forgotten in that trackless wasteland – if, just a few miles away, an aboriginal named Mosic had not had a strange dream.

Mosic lived in an aboriginal settlement at Delissaville, across the bay from Darwin. An expert tracker, he was often called upon to help Jack Murray, the settlement's superintendent, to rescue shot-down airmen from the jungle on Australia's north-west coast.

On the sixth morning after Lieutenant Johnston parachuted from his blazing P–40, Murray received a message from Air Command HQ in Darwin which stated that an American figher pilot had been shot down about 20 miles (32 km) south-west of Delissaville. Murray could not know that the downed pilot in this case was not Johnston, who had already been given up for dead by Air Command; neither could he know that there had been a mistake, and that the airman he was setting out to find had actually come down north-east of the settlement.

Together with Mosic and a second aboriginal, Murray climbed into his launch and set course south-westwards along the coast – in the wrong direction, as far as Air Command was concerned, but in a direction that would lead him unknowingly to the missing Lieutenant Johnston.

As they cruised along the coast, scanning the mouths of the dozens of small creeks that broke up the shoreline in the hope that they might see a dinghy or some sign of life, Murray noticed that Mosic seemed uneasy. Suddenly, the aboriginal jumped to his feet and pointed to the mouth of one creek. Excitedly, he announced that only last night he had dreamed about the place, and that in his dream they had sailed up the waterway.

Murray never underestimated the aborigines, and knew from exper-ience that their 'hunches' often turned out to be right. Anyway, they had to start searching somewhere – and the creek seemed to be as good a place as any. They turned upstream, following the creek under an arch of trees through which the sun's light filtered in a green glow. From time to time, what looked like a brown log suddenly came to life on the bank and slid into the water. But the crocodiles didn't worry the three men. If you left them alone, they usually left you alone. The mosquitoes and leeches were the real enemies.

They had gone about a mile upstream when suddenly, appar-ently for no reason at all, Mosic shoved the tiller hard over and

brought the launch to a stop among the mangroves near the bank. Round-eyed, he told Murray that in his dream, this was the place – the exact place – where they had halted. Murray stared hard at the aboriginal, trying to decide what to do next. It was then that they heard the cry – a hoarse, weak cry for help, coming out of the depths of the swamp.

The three men jumped from the launch and plunged into the wilder-ness. The aborigines unerringly picked their way over the hard ground that led through the waste of roots and black mud, following the cries for help. Just 200 yards from the creek, clinging to the fork of a tree, they found Lieutenant Johnston – and not before time.

He was bearded and filthy, his face and arms bloated to twice their size by the bites of swarms of insects. He collapsed in tears when he saw the three men, babbling deliriously about the slimy horrors he had seen crawling a few feet below his refuge. The rescuers helped him back to the launch and gave him a mug of scalding tea, laced with rum. A few minutes later, he was able to sit up and talk coherently.

Murray was incredulous when Johnston introduced himself and told the superintendent that he had been in the swamp for six days, until he suddenly realized that this was not the airman they had been sent out to find. His incredulity deepened when the American told him that – having no idea that the creek was so close at hand – he had been about to finish himself off, unable to endure the torment of insect bites any longer.

Safely back at Delissaville, Murray radioed Air Command HQ and learned that the other airman had been picked up by someone else. The duty officer at AHQ was astonished when Murray told him that Johnston was alive, and asked how Murray had known where to look.

Rather lamely, Murray told him that pure chance had led him to the American. It was only years after the war that he revealed the truth – that Johnston had owed his life to an aboriginal tracker's mysterious dream.

He was not alone. Numerous Allied pilots, brought down in the track-less wastes of northern Australia, had cause to be grateful for the native trackers' almost uncanny powers. For some pilots it became a superstition; they carried aboriginal charms into the air with them, or had images of aboriginal deities painted on their aircraft. One such was the Bunyip, the fearsome aboriginal symbol of death, which adorned the nose of the P–40 flown by Lieutenant Edgar Ball of the 49th Group's 7th Squadron.

BELOW
American pilot poses alongside the fearsome Bunyip deity painted on his aircraft.

ABOVE

Aborigines performing a tribal dance, with ritual markings on their bodies.

It was a strange meeting of two cultures, but years later, an even stranger tale was told of how the Australian aborigines put their ancient magic to work to protect a man who – just like the men who had flown into action time after time against the Japanese – they regarded almost as godlike.

At 9.47 in the morning of 20 February, 1962, a huge Atlas booster rocket thundered skywards from Cape Canaveral, carrying American astronaut Colonel John Glenn into space inside the Mercury capsule Friendship 7. Nearly 11 months after Russia's Major Yuri Gagarin had hurtled round the world in his Vostok spacecraft, John Glenn had begun the 80,428-mile journey through space that was to make him the first American to carry out a complete orbit of the earth.

The lift-off was perfect. The capsule separated from the booster rocket, coasted into orbit and raced on over the Atlantic. As he

was crossing Africa, Glenn carried out a number of tests to see how his body reacted to the state of zero gravity; he reported that he experienced no ill-effects at all.

Out over the Indian Ocean, the Africa far behind, Friendship 7 plunged abruptly into the shadows of the night. On it sped, over darkened Australia, when suddenly Glenn saw a blaze of light far beneath him. It was the city of Perth, whose people had turned on all their lights to provide a beacon for the astronaut. Glenn was grateful for the friendly sight; it made his journey seem less lonely.

Shortly before dawn, as the capsule was approaching Hawaii, Glenn looked out of the observation port and saw something that was both startling and unexpected. At first, he thought he was

looking at a field of stars – and then he saw that the spacecraft was passing through a belt consisting of thousands of tiny particles, yellowish-green in colour and as brilliant as fireflies. He could not explain the luminous 'snowflakes'; neither could the scientists on the ground.

It was when the capsule was over Guaymas, Mexico, near the end of its first orbit that things started to go wrong. Glenn found that one of the small jets that made up the capsule's attitude control system, essential to maintaining a stable trajectory, was not working properly.

As a result, Friendship 7 began to yaw to the right. Glenn was forced to take over manual control, and for almost the rest of the trip he flew the capsule by hand, steadying it by gentle use of the attitude jets whenever it began to roll. A few minutes later, he reported that the spacecraft was under full control once more.

However, Glenn's troubles were only just beginning. Minutes after the astronaut and Mercury Control had made the decision that all systems were 'go' for a third orbit, a warning light flashed on an instrument panel in Mercury Control. It meant that the fibreglass heat shield on Friendship 7 had worked loose – and if the shield became completely detached from the capsule before or during re-entry, both the capsule and Glenn would disintegrate in a soundless gush of flame.

As the capsule sped on, other tracking stations around the globe also picked up the signal. After minutes of terse consultation with his team of experts, Mercury Operations Director Walter Williams advised Glenn that if the shield really was loose, he would have to change the re-entry procedure if he was to have even a slim chance of survival.

Normally, the retro-rocket pack, which was attached to the capsule by three metal bands, was jettisoned as soon as the rockets were fired. But if the pack was left in place, the bands might just be strong enough to hold the shield in place – and by the time the

ABORIGINAL GODS

The age-old Australian aboriginal myths are both powerful and richly imaginative. The whole of creation, they say, was fathered by a mythical being who arose from the sea. An emu's egg, thrown into the sky, set fire to a pile of sticks and became the sun; alternatively, other tribes in central Australia believe that the sun is an old woman dressed in a red kangaroo skin, who climbs into the sky each day and then descends in the evening to visit the land of the dead. The aboriginal gods are functional, simple beings who hold sway over the hills and deserts, waterholes and all the living creatures that inhabit the southern continent.

ABOVE LEFT
Reproduction of an Aboriginal cave painting, depicting a spirit. Many have been eager to cite this sketch as evidence that extra-terrestrials have landed in the Bush!

LEFT
An aboriginal family butchering a kangaroo, their main food source.

heat of re-entry burned the pack away, Williams hoped that the capsule would have descended deeply enough into the earth's atmosphere for the air pressure to keep the shield in position.

Carefully, Glenn manoeuvred the capsule into the correct attitude for re-entry. The retros were fired and the spacecraft arced down into the upper layers of the atmosphere, surrounded by a brilliant and – to the astronaut – terrifying firework display as the retro-pack burned away.

Minutes later John Glenn and Friendship 7 splashed down safely in the Atlantic, to the relief of all concerned. Later, it was discovered that the heat-shield warning had been false, triggered by a faulty instrument.

Soon after his return from space, the astronaut told newsmen of the miracles he had seen in space: the patterns of light and colour that weaved their bands over the earth's service, and the mysterious 'snowflakes' that no-one could explain.

And yet – as Glenn flew over Australia, aboriginal magic had been at work. Near the tracking station at Parkes, members of an aboriginal clan – some of whom worked as labourers at the station – had lit a big fire in the desert, and invoked their gods to protect the lonely man high above the earth. Sparks from the fire whirled up into the darkness on eddies of warm air as the aborigines chanted their ancient rituals – sparks that resembled the luminous particles the astronaut had seen.

From the mists of the Dreamtime, ancient spells had combined with modern technology to bring John Glenn safely home.

ABOVE
A gathering of aborigines in Tasmania, 1859. Painting by Robert Dowling, Queen Victoria Museum.

CHAPTER 11

The Dead Who Wouldn't Lie Down

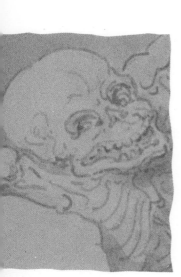

The afternoon of 9 August, 1812, was almost un-
bearably hot. The harsh sunlight glittered on the
placid waters of Oistin's Bay, Barbados, and shim-
mering waves of heat danced on the white,
dusty road that led up to Christ Church. The
sombre procession wound its way slowly between the graves in
the churchyard, moving in time with the heavy toll of the bell.
Sweat streamed down the faces of the bearers as they laboured
under the burden of the oak coffin.

It was a big funeral. Almost everyone who held a position of
any significance in Barbados was there, the ladies fanning themselves vigorously, the men red-faced and sweltering in formal black
clothing. A big funeral for a big man, for no-one would deny that
in stature at least, the Honourable Thomas Chase had been quite a
size – and quite a weight too, as the pall-bearers found to their
cost. Chase had not been a particualry wealthy or influential man,
though he had held a few minor government posts on the island,
but it was as a merchant – and an honest one, which was rare in
those days – that he would be remembered and respected.

LEFT
*The beauty of the evening sky over
Barbados. The island's tranquility
was troubled by strange happenings.*

FACING PAGE
*An artist captures the shock on
Viscount Combermère's face, as he
discovers that the Chase family tomb
has once again been desecrated by
mysterious forces.*

The cortege moved towards the Chase family tomb, a partly-buried vault of heavy stone that already contained the bodies of three members of the family; Mrs Thomasina Goddard, Chase's sister, who had been laid to rest there in July 1807; Mary Ann Chase, Thomas's little daughter, who had been buried in February 1808; and Dorcas Chase, an older daughter, whose funeral had taken place just a month earlier, on 6 July, 1812.

A small party moved forward to lift the heavy stone slab that covered the vault. They moved it aside with considerable difficulty, allowing a shaft of sunlight to penetrate the darkness below. And at that moment, what had until then been a perfectly ordinary funeral suddenly turned into a horrifying mystery. They recoiled from the vault's entrance, stark fear stamped on their black faces. Their task should have been to carry the coffin down the short flight of steps into the vault, but they flatly refused to do so. Curious to find out why they were so terrified, a few people pushed forward to peer into the vault – and got the shock of their lives.

A month earlier, when Dorcas Chase had been laid to rest, the three coffins in the vault had been tucked tidily away in their respective niches. But now Mary Ann's little coffin was standing on end against the far wall of the vault, and the others were lying on the floor, tumbled out of their places.

After the initial shock had worn off, the funeral of Thomas Chase went ahead as planned. The other three coffins were carefully returned to their places, and Thomas's lead-lined casket was laid beside them. Afterwards, the entrance stone was replaced and sealed around the edges with cement.

The authorities in Barbados were seriously disturbed by the incident. On the face of it, it looked as though someone had broken into the grave in an attempt to rob the bodies – and grave-robbing was a crime punishable by death. Everyone who worked in or near the cemetery was thoroughly questioned, but with no result. And there was no escaping the fact that the coffins themselves had not been tampered with; they bore no marks in evidence of any attempt to break them open.

But the authorities were taking no chances. They ordered that the seals on all the vaults in the churchyard were to be inspected regularly – at least twice a day. For four years this routine was strictly observed, and during all that time nothing happened that could be classed even remotely as out of the ordinary. Not, that is, until the funeral of another member of the Chase family – a young boy named Samuel Ames.

Before the vault was opened, a delegation composed of church and civic dignitaries examined the seal around the slab. It was

intact, and clearly had not been tampered with in any way. But when the slab was lifted aside, the astonished officials found that the coffins were scattered around the vault's interior, just as they had been at Thomas Chase's funeral. Only one coffin was still in its place: that of Mrs Goddard, who had been the vault's first occupant. Thomas Chase's coffin, which was so heavy that it had taken eight men to lift it, was lying on its side at the far end of the vault, 6ft (1.8m) from its original place.

Once again, the coffins were replaced in their niches – and once again, the tomb was sealed. This time, however, the authorities placed an armed guard outside the vault, with instructions to shoot any unauthorized person who approached it. The authorities might have done better to save the expense of paying the guard's wages, because absolutely nothing happened. Yet when the tomb was opened just a couple of months later to admit another member of the Chase family, the coffins inside were tumbled about haphazardly, just as before.

Shortly afterwards, a new governor arrived in Barbados. He was Field Marshal Viscount Combermere, a leather-featured old campaigner who had seen death too many times to be frightened of it, or by fantastic stories of coffins that jumped around. Nevertheless, Lord Combermere was an intelligent man, and he quietly set about gathering as much information as possible on the Chase vault mystery. He was convinced that something strange had occurred in the vault; there were far too many responsible witnesses for him to believe otherwise. What he intended to do, in his grim, soldierly way, was to find out just what it was that caused coffins to move about in a sealed vault – and to put a stop to it once and for all.

On 17 July, 1819, the bell of Christ Church tolled for another funeral; that of a certain Mrs Clark, another of Thomas Chase's sisters. More out of curiosity than anything else, the Governor attended the funeral – and was standing right outside the Chase vault when it was opened.

If Lord Combermere had managed to convince himself that the whole business was eyewash after all, he was in for a shock. For when his eyes grew accustomed to the gloom inside the freshly-opened vault, he saw that the coffins were stacked in a loose pile in the centre of the floor.

As soon as the coffins had been replaced and the funeral of Mrs Clark was over, the Governor and his men went to work. First of all, they examined the interior of the vault for hidden entrances – and found none. Then they scattered fine ash over the floor and up the steps of the vault, in the hope that any intruder – supernatural or not – would leave footprints behind. Finally, the Governor personally supervised the sealing of the vault with cement.

The vault remained sealed for nine months, until April 1820 – a couple of weeks before Lord Combermere was due to relinquish his post as Governor of Barbados. Before he returned to England, the old soldier was determined to find out if there had been any further disturbances in the tomb – and, on the pretext that unexplained noises had been heard in the cemetery, he ordered the vault to be opened for inspection.

The cement seal was removed; the great stone slab was pushed aside. The ashes that Combermere's men had scattered over the floor of the vault were undisturbed and bore no traces of any intruder. But the coffins lay in jumbled disorder just the same.

Lord Combermere went back to England, completely baffled. Later, he wrote a full account of the strange events in the Chase tomb in his memoirs.

For the survivors of the Chase family, the disturbance discovered in April 1820 was the last straw. They had the bodies removed and buried in another cemetery. The vault was sealed for the last time; it still stands today, worn and scarred by the weather, guarding its weird secret.

However, the removal of the bodies did nothing to dispel the sinister aura that had grown around Christ Church and its graveyard. In 1831, the church itself was destroyed by a storm – and just over 100 years later, its successor was ravaged by fire. Then, in August 1943, came another mystery. The 24th of that month was an important occasion for the Freemasons of Barbados. The vault of Sir Ewan MacGregor was to be opened – and in that same tomb lay the body of Alexander Irvine, who had founded the Craft or Barbados before his death in 1841.

The MacGregor vault, too, was underground and built from thick stone. It was sealed by a heavy door at the foot of a short flight of steps, and the door itself had been bricked up solidly.

Carefully, piece by piece, workmen removed the brickwork. Behind it, there seemed to be some sort of obstruction in the doorway. A few minutes later, the men saw what it was: a lead-sheathed coffin, standing on its end and leaning against the brickwork. As more bricks were removed, the coffin slid down until it was lying on its side on the floor.

Entering the vault, the Masons peered around in the gloom. The coffin on the floor contained the body of Sir Ewan MacGregor, and how it had come to be standing on end in the doorway was a complete mystery. But there was an even greater enigma – for there was no sign at all of either the coffin or the body of Alexander Irvine. Yet he had certainly been there 100 years earlier when the vault was sealed – and the seal had not been touched since that time.

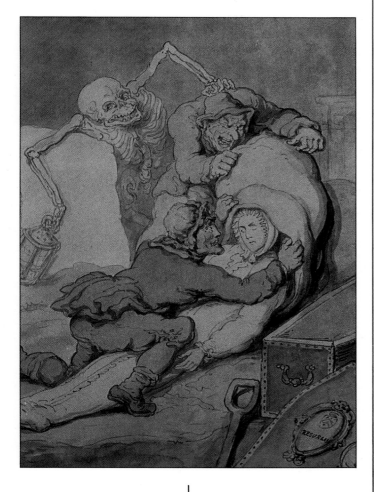

FACING PAGE, TOP
Field Marshal Viscount Combermère, the Governor of Barbados who tried to solve the 'jumping coffin' mystery.

ABOVE
The Resurrectionists by Thomas Rowlandson. Grave-robbing was, however, discounted as impossible in the Barbados case.

Barbados appears to have had more than its fair share of 'moving coffin' phenomena, but similar cases have been recorded in other parts of the world. One particularly famous British case involved the ancient tomb of the French family at Stanton in Suffolk, a few miles northeast of Bury St Edmunds. When the vault was opened in 1755, the records of the parish church tell us, the coffins inside were found to be lying in a state of disorder. One big lead-sheathed coffin, which required eight men to lift it, was lying on its side at the opposite end of the vault from its original position. There was absolutely nothing that might account for the disturbance. The coffins were replaced and the vault was sealed again.

But perhaps the strangest and most unnerving 'jumping coffin' mystey occurred on the Estonian island of Saaremaa, which lies across the entrance to the Gulf of Riga. A hundred years ago, there was only one town on the windswept island; Arensburg, now renamed Valjala. Arensburg was the home of the wealthy Buxhoewden family, whose private chapel and vault lay beside the road that ran past the town's little cemetery.

In 1844, several travellers reported that their horses had gone into a state of wild panic as they passed the Buxhoewden vault, for no apparent reason. Some people claimed that they had heard strange rumbling noises coming from the tomb.

Matters came to a head one Sunday morning, when a dozen horses tethered outside the Buxhoewden chapel suddenly began to rear and plunge alarmingly. Six of them collapsed and died on the spot, blood streaming from their nostrils.

Thoroughly alarmed, the owners of the animals sent a deputation to the local clergy, who in turn approached the Buxhoewden family and asked permission to open the vault. At first, the Buxhoewdens flatly refused, saying that the strange happenings were the work of some enemy. But at last they relented; wild rumours had begun to circulate and it was whispered that the family was in league with the Devil. The Buxhoewdens had nothing to hide, and they knew that no-one could possibly have got into their vault. The door was sealed with lead. So they agreed to the vault being opened, hoping that it would silence the wagging tongues.

But no-one, least of all the Buxhoewdens, was prepared for the sight that the opened tomb revealed. All the coffins were piled in an untidy heap in the middle of the floor. The coffins were carefully replaced and the vault was sealed. It was not opened again until six weeks later, when an elderly member of the family died. The coffins were again found to be scattered around the tomb.

No-one could offer a rational explanation. No valuables were missing from the bodies, so the disturbance was not the work of grave-robbers. And in any case, there was absolutely no way into the tomb except by way of the sealed door.

The tomb was sealed once more – and just a week later, passers-by heard more strange rumblings coming from the interior. Resignedly, the Buxhoewdens authorized the vault to be opened yet again, knowing full well what they would find. The coffins were replaced, ashes were scattered over the floor of the tomb, the vault was sealed and prayers were read over it. Then everyone went away, leaving guards around the vault and hoping fervently that the coffins would stay in their places this time.

They did not, and the Buxhoewdens, unable to stand it any longer, had the bodies of their ancestors removed and laid to rest in a quiet, secluded corner of the churchyard. Like the Chase family, they had found to their cost that whatever strange, unnatural force had picked on them for its plaything, it could be silenced only by an admission of total surrender.

BELOW

Baron von Schrenck-Notzing, who attempted to provide a scientific theory of psychokinesis, experimented in the 1920s with famous medium Stanislava Tomczyk. She is shown here levitating a rubber ball.

PSYCHOKINESIS

A modern scientific explanation for the 'jumping coffin' phenomenon is that it might have been caused by psychokinesis, the movement or materialization of objects by the mind of a living person. There are many recorded instances of the phenomenon, and science is only just coming to grips with the study of it. It is triggered by rare individuals who usually have a history of such manifestations. In 1974, for example, a teenager called Matthew Manning of Cambridge, England, inadvertently produced a sensational example of psychokinesis when, while his abilities were being scientifically tested, he moved dozens of objects including furniture from one part of his home to another, purely by the power of his mind.

CHAPTER 12

Witchcraft Today

BELOW
*Evidence of Satanic activity
discovered by the British Psychic and
Occult Society in the autumn of 1971
at a disused chapel in Highgate
cemetery, north London.*

Walter Binsted was puzzled. It was a cold evening in December, 1963, and as a bellringer of many years' standing Binsted knew that there should be no-one in the belfry of the little church in the village of Westham, Sussex, at this late hour. But there was no mistaking the dim light that shone from the belfry window. Binsted decided that he ought to investigate. Going up to the church door, he found it unlocked. He opened it and went inside.

What he saw stopped him dead in his tracks. At the far end of the church, which was dimly lit by candles placed in the shape of a cross on the chancel floor near the alter, stood four men. As Binsted watched, the man who stood nearest the altar, chanting, began to dance, slowly at first and then with increasing tempo. He was joined by his companions, until – as Binsted put it later – 'they seemed to be dancing around those candles like creatures from hell itself'.

At that moment, Binsted reached out and switched on the lights. The men stopped in the middle of their dance and rushed towards him, shouting angrily. Binsted turned and ran to the village hall, where he knew he would find the vicar. Minutes later,

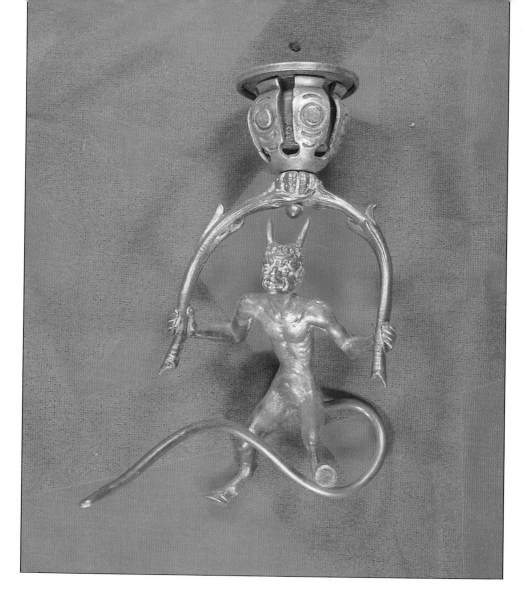

ABOVE
Demonic candle-holder and pentacle flag, used to conjure up Satan in modern black magic rituals.

he returned with the vicar and a small party of volunteers. As they reached the door, they ran headlong into the four strangers who came charging out of the church. Knocking down one of the men standing next to the vicar and scattering the others, they jumped into a car parked some distance down the road and drove off at high speed before anyone could stop them.

When the police arrived, the candles were still burning in the church. Nothing had been stolen or damaged, but spittle dripped from the crucifix on the altar, which had been desecrated.

The Westham affair awakened the public to the fact that there was a resurgence of Satanism and witchcraft in England. Just three weeks after the clandestine ceremony in the church, headstones and carved figures were damaged in the churchyard of St Nicholas, Bramber, near Brighton, and black magic symbols were chalked on the doors of the church. Experts who examined the damage and symbols affirmed that they were not the work of mere vandals, as had originally been suspected, but of someone with a definite knowledge of the Black Art.

RIGHT

Ancient Celtic cross at Perranporth, Cornwall. Such Christian symbols have served for centuries to guard travellers against dark forces.

So much has been written about the resurgence of witchcraft and black magic in Britain that it is very hard to say where fact ends and fantasy begins. However, it should be made clear that not all witches are 'black'. The members of the majority of modern witches' covens are ordinary people who sincerely believe in the 'Old Religion' and who try to recapture some of its lost arts and secrets. Witchcraft in itself is not inherently evil; it is only the perverted minds of some practitioners that make it so.

The principle behind black magic has changed very little in 1,000 years. It is simply the art of channelling the hidden powers of the human mind for evil purposes. The black witch, the satanist, is an instinctive lover of evil and will stop at nothing to achieve his purpose. In every satanist, there is a little of the psychology that goes into the making of a murderer.

There are black covens all over Britain. Most are in the big cities, but one meets in Sherwood Forest and there is another in Brighton which has several well-known figures among its members. The

FACING PAGE

One English black coven meets amid the twisted and gnarled oaks of Sherwood Forest, famous for the Robin Hood legend.

methods of becoming a black witch vary from coven to coven; making the initial contact is not difficult, for the strange mentality that urges a person to dabble in black witchcraft gravitates towards others of a similar mind.

Once contact has been established, the interested party receives visitors in the shape of one or two members of the coven, who question him carefully in order to find out whether his interest is genuine. If the applicant does appear genuine, he will then serve a probationary period of 13 months, during which he will be instructed in the basic teachings of the cult. He will also be asked to undergo a series of tests; these vary depend-ing on the cult to which the candidate belongs, but usually include the desecration of churches and churchyards and perhaps grave-robbing.

After the probationary period, the candidate is admitted to the order as a novice. Next comes the degree of Zelator – and the student has a prospect, after many years of study, of attaining the grade of Magus. The highest grade is Ipsissimus; only a handful of adepts ever reach it. Only an Ipsissimus can celebrate a Black Mass.

The rite of the Black Mass itself has varied very little in centuries, with the exception that cannibalism is seldom practised nowadays. The reason is that human beings for sacrifice are hard to come by; once, if a child disappeared, there was very little anyone could do about it – but today, the disappearance of a child would result in a massive manhunt, and the satanists are desperately anxious to keep their activities well clear of any interference by the police. Today, it is a dog, cat or black cock that is sacrificed.

There is a good deal of evidence to support this. A few years ago, for example, a chalice was stolen from a church in Dorset. Several days later it reappeared on the altar, stained with blood that was believed to have come from a black cock, discovered in the churchyard with its throat cut. On another occasion, a newly-severed pig's head was found between three wooden crosses on Tooting Bec Common, London. Fetishes in the form of sheep's hearts, studded with 13 thorns, are frequently found nailed to the doors of churches.

Superstitious rubbish? Just a few years ago, that would have been the verdict of most people – but not any more. Even though the study of parapsychology is barely out of the crawling stage, it is now widely believed that thought-waves can be concentrated and directed, that their power is virtually limitless and that they can bring about structural changes in matter. The Black Mass is instrumental in strengthening the mental force of the people who celebrate it, and their emotions generate a vast amount of energy.

The Black Mass, in fact, is the most powerful generator of energy in witchcraft. It has to be, for more mental force is required to work evil than to work good. The rituals of white covens, however, fulfil the same purpose – the difference being that they start with the inflexible rule that magic must never be used to injure anyone. Every case that might merit the use of magic is brought before the coven; if there is any possibility of the power 'going astray', the idea is abandoned.

BELOW
Rangda, the dreaded widow, who is impersonated in the Baron's Dance. Symbols such as this – from Indonesia – also feature in European witchcraft today.

FACING PAGE
The goat, worshipped at the Black Sabbath, may have originated in the idol Baphomet, allegedly worshipped by the Knights Templar. It was venerated as a symbol of fecundity in Egypt, and was transformed by Judeo-Christianity into the 'Devil'.

One of Britain's leading researchers into witchcraft and magic, Gerald Yorke, claimed to have had first-hand experience of the power that can be unleashed by certain rituals. As a student at Cambridge University, he became interested in the occult and somehow got hold of the ancient ritual used for invoking Thoth, the Egyptian god of wisdom and inspiration. Thoth appeared, though in what manner Yorke would never divulge. He was so staggered, however, that he swore never again to conduct an experiment of this kind.

From the moment he enters a coven, either black or white, most of a witch's time is devoted to developing his personal contribution to the collective mental power of the coven. Every ritual, from the moment of initiation, takes him a further step along the path of psychic development. White covens, having nothing to hide, have never made any real secret of their rites and teachings; it is a good deal easier, for example, to find out the initiation rites of a witches' coven than it is to discover the initiation rites of Freemasonry.

The initiation rite varies only in minor detail from coven to coven. First of all a circle 9ft (3m) in diameter, is traced on the ground with the sacred black-handled knife, and then marked out in charcoal or chalk. At the centre of the circle stands the altar, bearing the ritual symbols of witchcraft. The sacred knife, symbolizing air; the wand, a symbol of fire and masculinity; a cauldron, symbolizing water and the Great Mother; and the pentacle, the symbol of earth. Other instruments might include a sword and a cord, which is the symbol of the universal spirit or force that binds all matter together.

FACING PAGE
A modern, surrealistic view of the Devil.

THE SABBATH

The origin of the word 'Sabbat' is obscure. Some sources say that it comes from Sabazius, who was identified with Dionysus and Zeus and is also said to be the same as the Jewish Oreb, Lord God of Sabaoth. Some evidence for this lies in the fact that the first Jews who settled in Rome were expelled under a law which forbade worshippers of Sabazius to live in the city. On the other hand, there may be a simpler explanation. In the early years of Christianity in Europe, priests would hold their services on days when the people were free from their toil – rest days. The word Shabhath, which means rest day in Hebrew, was imported and transformed. It should be remembered that before the Greek language exerted its influence on the Christian Church, Christians (from the Greek Christos) were called Jews of the Nazarene Sect, and Hebrew would feature in the language of the early wandering priests. The word Sabbath, or Sabbat, came to mean a religious gathering, applicable to both pagan and Christian ceremonies.

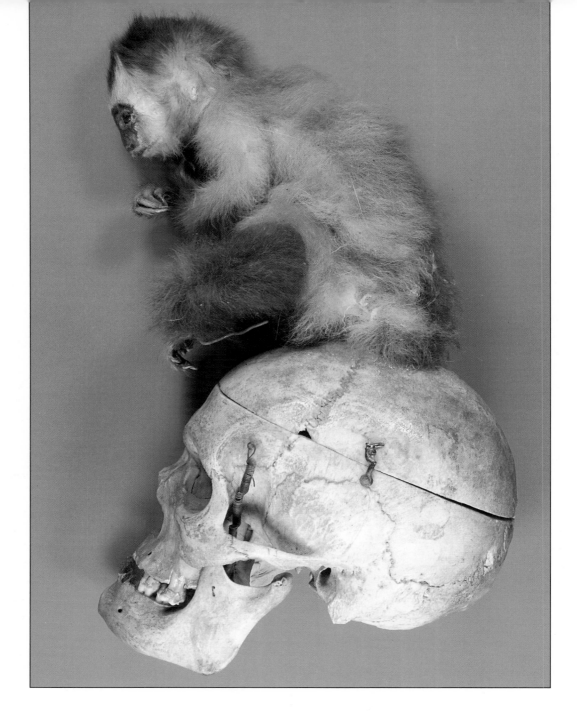

Candles are lit on the altar and everything is sanctified by sprinkling salt and water. The members of the coven walk slowly round the circle, chanting an invocation to the Mighty Ones – the ancient gods of North, South, East and West. The coven leader then touches the breast of the candidate, who is standing outside the circle, with the point of the sacred knife, intoning that it is better to die by the knife than enter the craft with fear in the heart. The candidate replies with the password: 'Perfect love and perfect trust.' He then enters the circle and his hands and feet are ceremonially bound with cord. After being presented to the Mighty Ones at each point of the compass, the candidate, with hands still bound, is led back to the altar where his feet are tied once again.

Kneeling, he swears that he will be faithful to the craft forever. Then he is purified by the High Priestess, who strikes him 40 times with a ceremonial scourge. Once, this was a painful ordeal; today, however, the scourging is limited to a series of gentle flicks. Some covens do not use it at all. Following the scourging, the candidate swears an oath of allegiance to his brothers and sisters of the craft. Afterwards, he is consecrated with oil, wine and a ritual kiss. He is then presented with the tools of the craft: the black-handled knife, a white-handled knife, a sword, a censer, a cauldron, scourge and wand. He is also given a white cord, the symbol of the first degree of initiation, and is proclaimed a novice. After this, the members of the coven sit in a circle and eat a ritual meal.

FACING PAGE

*This bizarre union of skull and
monkey was supposed, by master
sorcerer Aleister Crowley, to be
effective in summoning up evil forces.*

RIGHT

*A Cornish witch, Cait Sidh,
celebrating a Sabbath.*

To most people, a witch's spell means a curse of some kind; but spells work just as efficiently for good as for evil, and today the power of the witches – black covens apart – is mainly directed towards healing and extending help, by magical means, to those who ask for it and genuinely need it. Many believe that the power can also be used to influence the weather; there is a legend that it was the efforts of witches, acting in unison all over England, that caused the storm which destroyed the Spanish Armada. More recently, it has been claimed that witches in Britain used their powers collectively to influence Hitler – which resulted in his decision to postpone the invasion of Britain in 1940. (Though the Royal Air Force and the Battle of Britain might have had something to do with it!) Nevertheless, there is plenty of evidence that Hitler was influenced in all his major decisions by the astrologers and magicians with whom he had surrounded himself, and whose opinions he valued highly.

One thing that is immediately apparent about the Old Religion in Britain – and presumably elsewhere – today is that it is badly uncoordinated. Most white covens agree on the basic principles of the art, but no two covens practise it in exactly the same way. Many witches see their art as a great potential source of good in combating the evil influences that are at work in the world today, but they feel that, like almost every other Western religion, the art has fallen behind in the general march of progress. Unlike most religions, however, which rely on vague and often misinterpreted mysteries for their teachings, the laws and aims of the Old Religion are clear and well-defined.

Looking back through history, the fearful persecution suffered by witches was in itself an admission of belief in their powers. The unfortunate thing was that the persecutors failed to realize that the majority of witches operated in the cause of good and not evil. It was the old story of the notoriety of a comparative few bringing harm to the many. The word 'witch' itself, which comes from the old Anglo-Saxon word *wicca*, meaning wise one, has quite wrongly become a symbol of evil. In ancient times, long before the purges of the Middle Ages, witches were respected members of the community; the fact that they came to be hated and feared may have been due to the 'closed circle' nature of their activities.

There is no danger in the modern world that a lack of understanding will lead to new persecutions. But the already widespread idea that witchcraft is nonsense, practised by the mentally deranged and perverts, could spread further. The fact that escapes most of its critics is that witchcraft, in its purest form, is a religion in the true sense of the word – some say the oldest religion in the world. Black witchcraft is simply a much perverted form of the basic religion, just as many outlandish sects have twisted the teachings of other major religions.

Today, witchcraft's most important ally is science – the science that is slowly beginning to accept the forms of perception that witches have been using for centuries. Stored away among the ancient rites and laws of witchcraft is the world's greatest fund of esoteric knowledge – knowledge that could be of immense value to the modern world, where the greatest battle is for control of the minds of men.

Index

Italic page numbers refer to illustration captions.

Picture Credits